WONDERS OF ZANZIBAR : A PREPARATION TRAVEL GUIDE

BELLA PHILLIPS

TABLE OF CONTENTS

Introduction

Zanzibar is an enchanting and culturally rich archipelago located in the Indian Ocean, just off the eastern coast of Tanzania. Comprising several islands, with the largest ones being Unguja and Pemba, Zanzibar is renowned for its stunning beaches, vibrant cultural heritage, and historical significance. This introduction will provide an overview of Zanzibar, touching on its history, geography, culture, and tourism.

Geography:
Zanzibar is situated approximately 25-50 kilometers off the Tanzanian coast. The archipelago is known for its crystal-clear waters, coral reefs, and white sandy beaches. The tropical climate, with distinct wet and dry seasons, makes it a popular destination for tourists seeking warm, sunny weather year-round.

History:
The history of Zanzibar is both fascinating and complex. It has been a melting pot of various cultures and civilizations due to its strategic location along major trade routes. Arab traders and Persians arrived on the islands as early as the 8th century, bringing with them Islam, which has had a lasting impact on the region. Zanzibar later became

the center of the Arab slave trade and a major trading hub for spices, particularly cloves.

In the 19th century, Zanzibar fell under the influence of the Sultan of Oman, who moved his court to the archipelago and ruled from there. Eventually, the British and the Sultanate of Zanzibar established a colonial presence. Zanzibar later gained independence from Britain in 1963 and merged with Tanganyika to form the United Republic of Tanzania in 1964.

Culture:
Zanzibar's cultural diversity is one of its most captivating features. The fusion of African, Arab, Indian, and European influences is evident in the local customs, language, cuisine, and architecture. Swahili is the primary language, and Islam is the dominant religion, with many beautiful mosques dotting the landscape.

The archipelago is famous for its traditional music and dance, with taarab music and ngoma dance being integral parts of Zanzibari culture. The intricate carvings, doors, and buildings in Stone Town, the historic center of Zanzibar City, reflect the rich architectural heritage of the region.

Tourism:
Zanzibar has become a popular tourist destination, known for its idyllic beaches, water sports, and vibrant marine life. Visitors can explore the colorful coral reefs through snorkeling and diving, go on spice tours to learn about the island's spice production, and enjoy boat trips to nearby islets.

Stone Town, a UNESCO World Heritage Site, is a must-visit destination for its winding streets, historical buildings, and lively markets. The cultural festivals like the Zanzibar International Film Festival (ZIFF) and the annual Mwaka Kogwa celebration offer unique opportunities to immerse in the local culture.

In conclusion, Zanzibar is a captivating destination that offers a rich blend of history, culture, and natural beauty. Whether you're interested in exploring its cultural heritage, relaxing on pristine beaches, or diving into the colorful underwater world, Zanzibar has something to offer every type of traveler. It's a place where the past and the present coexist harmoniously, making it a unique and enchanting destination in the Indian Ocean.

Chapter 1.

- *Welcome to Zanzibar*

"Welcome to Zanzibar" is a phrase that embodies the warm and inviting spirit of Zanzibar, an archipelago located off the coast of East Africa in the Indian Ocean. Zanzibar is a semi-autonomous region of Tanzania and is known for its breathtaking natural beauty, rich history, vibrant culture, and warm hospitality.

1. Geography and Location:
   Zanzibar consists of several islands, with the two main ones being Unguja and Pemba. It is situated approximately 25-50 kilometers off the Tanzanian coast. The archipelago is blessed with pristine white sandy beaches, crystal-clear waters, and lush tropical vegetation. The equatorial climate makes it a popular destination for sun-seekers and water sports enthusiasts.

2. History and Culture:
   Zanzibar has a complex and fascinating history. It was a major trading hub, known for its spices, ivory, and slaves. The islands have been influenced by various cultures over the centuries, including Arab, Indian, and European. This diverse heritage is evident in its architecture, cuisine, and way of life.

Stone Town, the historic core of Zanzibar City, is a UNESCO World Heritage site with narrow winding streets and beautifully carved doors, reflecting Swahili and Arab influences.

3. Spice Islands:

Zanzibar is often referred to as the "Spice Islands" due to its historical and current production of spices like cloves, cinnamon, and nutmeg. Visitors can explore spice plantations and learn about the cultivation and uses of these aromatic treasures.

4. Beaches and Marine Life:

The beaches of Zanzibar are a major draw for tourists. Pristine stretches of sand, such as Nungwi and Kendwa Beach on the north coast, offer opportunities for relaxation, water sports, and beachcombing. The surrounding coral reefs are a paradise for divers and snorkelers, with colorful marine life and underwater caves to explore.

5. Ecotourism:

Zanzibar is increasingly focused on sustainable and eco-friendly tourism. Visitors can engage in activities like turtle conservation projects, exploring Jozani Forest to see the rare red colobus monkeys, and supporting local communities through responsible tourism initiatives.

6. Cuisine:

Zanzibari cuisine is a fusion of various culinary traditions. Dishes often feature spices like cardamom, clove, and cinnamon. Seafood is a staple, and you can find local specialties like biryani and pilau rice, as well as delicious street food.

7. Hospitality and People:

Zanzibar is known for its friendly and hospitable people. The locals, predominantly of Swahili and Arab descent, are welcoming and often eager to share their culture and traditions with visitors.

8. Tourist Attractions:

In addition to its natural beauty, Zanzibar offers a range of attractions, including historical sites like the Palace Museum and the Old Fort, cultural experiences such as traditional music and dance performances, and outdoor activities like sailing, snorkeling, and kite surfing.

9. Festivals and Events:

Zanzibar hosts various festivals and events throughout the year, such as the Zanzibar International Film Festival (ZIFF) and the Sauti za Busara music festival, which showcase art, culture, and music.

In summary, "Welcome to Zanzibar" is an invitation to explore a unique and enchanting destination that offers a blend of history, culture, natural beauty, and warm hospitality. Whether you're looking for a beach getaway, an adventure in nature, or a cultural immersion, Zanzibar has something for every traveler.

- Getting to Zanzibar

Getting to Zanzibar, an exotic island paradise off the coast of Tanzania, is a dream for many travelers. Zanzibar, with its pristine beaches, rich cultural heritage, and vibrant marine life, is a sought-after destination. Here's a guide on how to get to Zanzibar:

1. Choosing the Right Time:
   - Zanzibar has a tropical climate, and the best time to visit is during the dry season, which typically falls between June and October. This period ensures pleasant weather and is ideal for various outdoor activities.

2. Arriving in Tanzania:
   - Most international travelers get to Zanzibar via Tanzania's mainland, either through Julius Nyerere International Airport in Dar es Salaam or

Kilimanjaro International Airport in Arusha. Make sure to secure a tourist visa for Tanzania if required.

3. Flights to Zanzibar:
   - The most common way to reach Zanzibar is by taking a flight from Tanzania's mainland to Abeid Amani Karume International Airport in Zanzibar. Several airlines operate daily flights from Dar es Salaam and other major Tanzanian cities to Zanzibar.

4. Direct International Flights:
   - Zanzibar also has direct international flights from a few select destinations, such as Nairobi (Kenya) and Doha (Qatar). Check with airlines like Qatar Airways, Kenya Airways, and Ethiopian Airlines for possible options.

5. Ferries from Dar es Salaam:
   - Another option is to take a ferry from Dar es Salaam to Zanzibar. The journey takes about 1.5 to 2 hours, and there are multiple ferry companies to choose from. Azam Marine and SeaLink are some popular options.

6. Entry Requirements:

- Ensure that you have a valid passport and any necessary visas for Tanzania and Zanzibar. Additionally, travelers should be prepared to pay an entry fee for Zanzibar upon arrival.

7. Transport on Zanzibar:
   - After arriving on the island, you can hire a taxi, use local minibus services (dala-dalas), or rent a car to reach your accommodation or explore the island. Alternatively, many resorts and hotels provide airport transfers.

8. Accommodation and Activities:
   - Zanzibar offers a wide range of accommodations, from luxury resorts to budget-friendly guesthouses. While there, don't miss out on exploring Stone Town, a UNESCO World Heritage Site, and enjoying water activities like snorkeling, diving, and spice tours.

9. Respecting Local Customs:
   - Zanzibar is predominantly Muslim, and it's essential to respect local customs and dress modestly, especially when outside beach areas. Alcohol is available but may be limited in some areas.

10. Safety and Health:

- Ensure you have the necessary vaccinations and take precautions against mosquito-borne diseases. Also, be mindful of your belongings and stay aware of your surroundings to ensure a safe and enjoyable stay.

In summary, getting to Zanzibar involves traveling to Tanzania's mainland and then making the final leg of the journey by air or sea. Once you arrive, you'll be captivated by the island's natural beauty, cultural richness, and warm hospitality, making your trip a memorable experience.

Chapter 2. Planning Your Trip

- Best Time to Visit

The best time to visit Zanzibar, a stunning tropical archipelago off the coast of Tanzania, depends on your preferences and what you want to experience during your trip. Zanzibar enjoys a tropical climate, and the island can be a year-round destination. However, there are distinct seasons that may influence your decision.

1. Dry Season (June to October): This is the most popular time to visit Zanzibar. The weather is dry and relatively cooler, making it perfect for outdoor activities and beach vacations. The average temperature during this period ranges from 24°C to 30°C (75°F to 86°F). It's an excellent time for water sports like snorkeling and diving as the visibility in the crystal-clear waters is at its best.

2. Shoulder Season (December to March): This period is another favorable time to visit Zanzibar. Although it's warmer and more humid, it offers good beach weather. However, occasional short rains can be expected. This season is also ideal for whale shark sightings, and it's a great time for those interested in exploring the rich marine life.

3. Long Rains (April and May): This is the rainy season in Zanzibar, and it's characterized by heavy rainfall. It's generally not recommended for tourists as the downpours can disrupt outdoor plans, cause flooding, and make some roads impassable. Accommodation prices may be lower during this period, but it's not the best time to enjoy the island's beauty.

4. Short Rains (November): This is the transitional period between the long rains and the dry season. While there can still be some rain, it's usually sporadic, and the island is less crowded. If you prefer a quieter experience and are willing to take the risk of some rain, this might be a good time for you to visit.

5. Festivals and Events: Zanzibar has various cultural events and festivals throughout the year, including the Zanzibar International Film Festival (July), the Mwaka Kogwa Festival (July), and the Sauti za Busara Music Festival (February). If you want to immerse yourself in the local culture, consider planning your trip around one of these events.

In summary, the best time to visit Zanzibar for most travelers is during the dry season, from June to

October, when the weather is pleasant and outdoor activities are at their best. However, the shoulder season and November also offer good experiences with fewer crowds and the opportunity to see unique wildlife. It's essential to consider your preferences and the activities you wish to undertake when planning your trip to this beautiful island.

- *Visa and Entry Requirements*

Visa and entry requirements in Zanzibar, a semi-autonomous region of Tanzania, are subject to change, so it's crucial to verify the latest information before planning your trip. Here's an overview of the visa and entry requirements for Zanzibar:

1. Passport Requirements:
   - To enter Zanzibar, your passport should be valid for at least six months beyond your intended departure date.

2. Visa Requirements:
   - Zanzibar typically follows the visa regulations of Tanzania. There are three main categories of visas for tourists:
      a. Tourist Visa: This is the most common visa for travelers visiting Zanzibar. It allows for a single entry and is typically valid for up to 90 days. You

can obtain a tourist visa upon arrival at the airport or seaport or through the Tanzanian embassy or consulate in your home country. It's recommended to check the latest visa fees and regulations before your trip.

b. e-Visa: Tanzania introduced an e-visa system that allows travelers to apply for a visa online before their trip. This can expedite the immigration process upon arrival.

c. Visa on Arrival: Some nationalities are eligible for visa on arrival. It's essential to check if your country is on the list of visa-exempt or visa-on-arrival countries and, if so, the conditions that apply.

3. Residence Permits:
 - If you plan to stay in Zanzibar for an extended period, such as for work, study, or volunteer programs, you may need to obtain a residence permit. The specific requirements and application process can be complex and vary based on your purpose of stay.

4. Yellow Fever Vaccination:

- Travelers coming from countries with a risk of yellow fever transmission may be required to show proof of yellow fever vaccination.

5. Customs Regulations:
- Be aware of the customs regulations in Zanzibar. Certain items, such as alcohol and tobacco, have limits on the quantity you can bring into the country without incurring additional taxes.

6. Visa Extensions:
- If you wish to extend your stay beyond the initial 90-day tourist visa, you may be able to apply for an extension, but this should be done through the Tanzanian immigration authorities.

7. Border Crossings:
- If you plan to enter Zanzibar via mainland Tanzania, ensure that you have the necessary visas and permits for both locations.

8. Exit Requirements:
- Before departing from Zanzibar, make sure to clear all exit requirements. Failure to do so might result in fines or complications during future visits.

9. Health and Travel Insurance:

- It is highly recommended to have health and travel insurance that covers medical emergencies, evacuation, and trip cancellation.

10. Local Regulations and Customs:
   - Respect local customs and laws. Zanzibar is predominantly Muslim, and you should dress modestly, especially when visiting religious sites.

Please note that these requirements can change, so it's essential to verify the latest information with the nearest Tanzanian embassy or consulate, as well as the official government websites before traveling to Zanzibar. Additionally, consider consulting with a travel agent or immigration expert for the most up-to-date guidance, especially if you have specific visa or residency needs.

- *Health and Safety Tips*

Health and safety tips are essential for anyone visiting or living in Zanzibar, as the island's unique environment and culture can present certain challenges. Here's a guide to staying safe and healthy in Zanzibar:

1. Vaccinations: Before traveling to Zanzibar, ensure you're up to date on routine vaccines. You may also need vaccines like Hepatitis A, Typhoid,

and Yellow Fever, depending on your home country and the areas you plan to visit.

2. Malaria Prevention: Malaria is prevalent in Zanzibar. Consult a healthcare professional for antimalarial medication and use mosquito nets, repellent, and wear long-sleeved clothing in the evenings.

3. Water and Food Safety: Drink bottled or purified water and avoid ice in drinks. Be cautious with street food; make sure it's cooked thoroughly and served hot.

4. Sun Protection: Zanzibar's tropical climate means strong sun exposure. Use sunscreen, wear a wide-brimmed hat, and stay hydrated to avoid heat-related illnesses.

5. Swimming Safety: Zanzibar boasts beautiful beaches, but always swim in designated areas and pay attention to local advice, as strong currents can be dangerous.

6. Respect Local Customs: Zanzibar is a predominantly Muslim society. Dress modestly, especially when visiting mosques, and respect local customs and traditions.

7. Insect Precautions: Protect against mosquito bites, not only for malaria but also to prevent diseases like dengue and chikungunya, which are also present.

8. Travel Insurance: Ensure you have travel insurance that covers medical emergencies, repatriation, and potential evacuation.

9. Transportation Safety: Be cautious when using local transportation. Ensure vehicles are in good condition and wear seat belts when available. Follow safety regulations for water taxis and ferries.

10. Healthcare: Zanzibar has some healthcare facilities, but for serious issues, it may be necessary to travel to the mainland or return home. Have access to a list of reputable clinics and doctors.

11. Language: Swahili is the primary language, so it's helpful to know some basic Swahili phrases for communication.

12. Currency and Safety: Beware of pickpocketing, especially in crowded areas. Carry only what you need and store valuables securely.

13. Environmental Concerns: Respect the fragile ecosystem of Zanzibar. Avoid touching or damaging coral reefs, and don't purchase products made from endangered species, like sea turtle shells or black coral.

14. Emergency Numbers: Know the local emergency numbers and have a working phone or communication device with you at all times.

15. Responsible Tourism: Choose responsible tour operators and accommodations that prioritise eco-friendly practices and support the local community.

By following these health and safety tips, you can ensure a safe and enjoyable visit to the stunning island of Zanzibar. Always stay informed, use common sense, and respect the local culture to have a memorable and secure experience.

- Packing Essentials

When traveling to Zanzibar, it's essential to pack wisely to ensure you have a comfortable and enjoyable trip. Zanzibar is a tropical paradise with beautiful beaches, historical sites, and vibrant local culture, so you'll want to be well-prepared for the unique experiences it offers. Here's a list of packing essentials for your trip to Zanzibar:

1. Passport and Visa: Ensure your passport is valid for at least six months from your entry date and that you have the necessary visas.

2. Travel Insurance: Purchase travel insurance that covers medical emergencies, trip cancellations, and lost belongings.

3. Lightweight Clothing: Pack lightweight, breathable clothing such as shorts, t-shirts, sundresses, and swimwear. Zanzibar has a hot and humid climate, so comfort is key.

4. Sarong or Cover-Up: These are handy for covering up when visiting more conservative areas or when transitioning from the beach to other activities.

5. Comfortable Footwear: Bring sandals, flip-flops, and water shoes for the beach. If you plan on doing some hiking or walking, consider closed-toe shoes as well.

6. Sun Protection: Sunscreen with high SPF, sunglasses, a wide-brimmed hat, and a rash guard

for water activities are crucial to protect yourself from the sun.

7. Insect Repellent: Malaria is present in some areas of Zanzibar, so pack an effective insect repellent and maybe even a mosquito net if you're staying in rustic accommodations.

8. Medications and First Aid: Bring any necessary prescription medications and a basic first-aid kit with essentials like band-aids, pain relievers, and anti-diarrheal medication.

9. Power Adapter and Voltage Converter: Zanzibar uses Type D and G electrical outlets with a voltage of 230V. Make sure to pack the right adapter and voltage converter if needed.

10. Reusable Water Bottle: Stay hydrated by carrying a reusable water bottle. You can refill it with purified water from larger containers available in many places.

11. Backpack or Day Bag: A small backpack is useful for day trips, hikes, and carrying essentials while exploring the island.

12. Camera and Accessories: Capture the beauty of Zanzibar with your camera. Don't forget extra memory cards and a waterproof case for water activities.

13. Toiletries: Pack your toiletries, including shampoo, conditioner, soap, and any specialty items you may need.

14. Travel Documents and Copies: Carry hard and digital copies of your travel documents, including flight itineraries, hotel reservations, and important contact numbers.

15. Cash and Cards: While there are ATMs in major towns, it's wise to carry some cash in both US dollars and Tanzanian shillings. Credit cards are widely accepted in larger establishments.

16. Snorkeling and Diving Gear: If you plan to explore Zanzibar's stunning underwater world, bring your snorkeling gear or inquire whether your accommodation provides it.

17. Travel Guide and Maps: A travel guidebook or digital maps can be invaluable for navigating the island and learning about its attractions.

18. Toilet Paper and Hand Sanitizer: These are handy for restrooms in more rural areas, which may not always have these amenities.

19. Respectful Clothing: When visiting Stone Town or local villages, it's respectful to dress modestly. Bring lightweight long-sleeved shirts and pants for such occasions.

20. Reusable Shopping Bag: Zanzibar has banned single-use plastic bags, so having a reusable shopping bag is environmentally friendly and practical.

Remember that packing light is key to enjoying your trip to Zanzibar. With these essentials, you'll be well-prepared for the tropical paradise and its unique experiences, from relaxing on the beach to exploring the island's culture and history.

Chapter 3. Zanzibar's Regions

- *Stone Town*

Stone Town, located in Zanzibar, is a place of rich historical and cultural significance. This UNESCO World Heritage Site is the old part of Zanzibar City and serves as a testament to the island's complex and diverse history. Let's explore its various aspects:

1. Historical Significance:
   - Stone Town's history dates back several centuries, with influences from Arab, Persian, Indian, and European traders, explorers, and colonial powers.
   - It was a major trading hub for spices, ivory, and slaves during the 19th century.

2. Architectural Marvel:
   - Stone Town is famous for its unique architecture, featuring intricately carved wooden doors, narrow winding streets, and historic buildings constructed from coral stone.
   - The fusion of Swahili, Arab, and European architectural styles is evident throughout the town.

3. Culture and People:

- The population of Stone Town is ethnically diverse, with a mix of Arab, African, Indian, and European influences.
- This cultural amalgamation is reflected in the cuisine, language, and traditions of the people.

4. Historic Buildings:
- Some notable structures include the House of Wonders, the Old Fort, the Sultan's Palace, and the Old Dispensary, all offering insights into Zanzibar's history.
- The architecture and design of these buildings are a unique blend of various influences.

5. Spice and Food Markets:
- Stone Town is famous for its vibrant markets, where you can find a variety of spices, fruits, vegetables, and seafood.
- It's also a fantastic place to sample Zanzibari cuisine, which incorporates a mix of flavors and ingredients from different cultures.

6. Museums and Cultural Sites:
- The Palace Museum and the Zanzibar Slave Chambers Museum provide historical context about the island's history and the transatlantic slave trade.

- Additionally, the Old Fort often hosts cultural events and exhibitions.

7. Waterfront and Beaches:
   - The waterfront area of Stone Town offers stunning views of the Indian Ocean and is a great place for a leisurely stroll.
   - Nearby beaches, such as Kendwa and Nungwi, are popular for their white sand and crystal-clear waters.

8. Festivals and Events:
   - Stone Town hosts various cultural festivals and events throughout the year, celebrating the island's diverse heritage.
   - The Zanzibar International Film Festival (ZIFF) and the Mwaka Kogwa Festival are notable examples.

9. Preservation Efforts:
   - Efforts have been made to preserve the unique architectural heritage of Stone Town, with organizations working to restore and maintain historic buildings.
   - Sustainable tourism practices aim to protect the cultural and natural assets of the area.

10. Zanzibar's Spice Trade:

- Zanzibar has a long history of spice cultivation, and Stone Town served as a hub for the spice trade. You can take spice tours to learn about the cultivation and processing of spices on the island.

In summary, Stone Town in Zanzibar is a living testament to the island's rich and complex history, with its unique architecture, diverse culture, and a blend of influences from around the world. It continues to be a captivating destination for travelers seeking a deeper understanding of Zanzibar's past and a taste of its vibrant present.

- *North Coast*

The North Coast of Zanzibar is a stunning and popular destination known for its pristine beaches, clear turquoise waters, and a relaxed atmosphere that draws travelers from all over the world. Here, I'll provide an overview of the North Coast of Zanzibar, including its attractions, activities, culture, and more.

Geography and Location:
The North Coast of Zanzibar is situated on the northernmost part of the Zanzibar Archipelago, which is part of Tanzania in East Africa. This region is characterized by a picturesque coastline along the

Indian Ocean, with its main town, Nungwi, at the tip of the island.

Beaches:
The most famous feature of the North Coast is its pristine beaches. Nungwi Beach, Kendwa Beach, and Matemwe Beach are some of the well-known stretches of sand in the region. These beaches are renowned for their soft, white sands and crystal-clear waters, making them perfect for sunbathing, swimming, and water sports.

Water Activities:
The North Coast is a paradise for water sports enthusiasts. Snorkeling, scuba diving, and swimming are popular activities thanks to the rich marine life, including colorful coral reefs and a variety of fish species. You can also find opportunities for sailing, fishing, and even traditional dhow boat cruises.

Nungwi Village:
Nungwi, the largest village on the North Coast, is a vibrant and culturally rich area. Visitors can explore the local fishing village, visit traditional markets, and interact with friendly locals. It's a great place to learn about the local Swahili culture and enjoy fresh seafood in beachfront restaurants.

Historical Sites:
Zanzibar has a fascinating history, and the North Coast has its share of historical sites. One notable attraction is the Nungwi Natural Aquarium, a conservation project where visitors can see sea turtles and learn about marine life conservation efforts. Additionally, you can visit the ruins of the Fukuchani Palace and other historical sites that provide insights into Zanzibar's past.

Nightlife:
While the North Coast maintains a relaxed vibe during the day, it comes alive at night. You'll find beach parties, bonfires, and reggae music events, making it a lively spot for those looking to enjoy Zanzibar's nightlife.

Luxury Resorts and Accommodation:
This region is home to some of the most luxurious and high-end resorts on the island. Many of these properties offer overwater bungalows and stunning ocean views, providing the perfect backdrop for a romantic getaway or a honeymoon.

Conservation Efforts:
Zanzibar is known for its conservation initiatives, and the North Coast is no exception. Various

organizations work towards protecting the marine life and ecosystems in the area, making it an eco-friendly destination for responsible travelers.

Best Time to Visit:
The North Coast is a year-round destination, but the dry season from June to October is typically considered the best time to visit due to pleasant weather conditions and low chances of rain.

In summary, the North Coast of Zanzibar offers a mix of natural beauty, cultural experiences, and recreational opportunities. Whether you seek a relaxing beach vacation, water adventures, or a taste of local culture, the North Coast has something for every traveler. Its breathtaking landscapes, vibrant culture, and warm hospitality make it a must-visit destination for anyone exploring East Africa.

- East Coast

Zanzibar is an archipelago located in the Indian Ocean, off the eastern coast of Tanzania. The island of Zanzibar is divided into two main regions: the East Coast and the West Coast. In this response, we will focus on the East Coast of Zanzibar and provide an overview of this region.

1. Geography and Location:

The East Coast of Zanzibar is known for its picturesque shoreline and stunning beaches. It stretches along the eastern side of the main island and faces the Indian Ocean. The region is characterized by its pristine white sandy beaches, lush vegetation, and turquoise waters.

2. Beaches and Natural Beauty:

The East Coast is renowned for its unspoiled beaches. The soft, powdery sand and clear waters make it an ideal destination for sunbathing, swimming, and water sports. Some of the popular beaches in this area include Paje Beach, Bwejuu Beach, and Jambiani Beach. These beaches offer a tranquil and idyllic setting for relaxation.

3. Water Activities:

The East Coast of Zanzibar is a haven for water sports enthusiasts. Visitors can enjoy activities such as snorkeling, scuba diving, kiteboarding, and sailing. The coral reefs in the Indian Ocean offer incredible opportunities for exploring marine life.

4. Cultural Experiences:

The East Coast also provides a chance to immerse oneself in the local culture. The villages in this region are home to friendly locals who are known for their warmth and hospitality. You can explore traditional Swahili villages, visit local markets, and engage in cultural exchanges.

5. Spices and Agriculture:
   Zanzibar, often referred to as the "Spice Island," is famous for its spice plantations. The East Coast has several spice farms where visitors can take guided tours to learn about the cultivation of spices like cloves, cinnamon, and nutmeg.

6. Historical Sites:
   Stone Town, the historic capital of Zanzibar, is easily accessible from the East Coast. This UNESCO World Heritage Site is known for its charming architecture, narrow streets, and historic buildings. Visitors can explore landmarks such as the House of Wonders and the Old Fort.

7. Accommodation:
   The East Coast offers a range of accommodation options, from luxury resorts to boutique hotels and guesthouses. Many of these establishments are located right on the beach, providing stunning ocean views and a relaxed atmosphere.

8. Marine Life and Conservation:

Zanzibar's East Coast is known for its efforts in marine conservation. The region is home to various marine protected areas and conservation projects aimed at preserving the rich biodiversity of the coral reefs and marine life.

9. Climate:
Zanzibar, including its East Coast, enjoys a tropical climate, making it a year-round destination. The dry season, which runs from June to October, is particularly popular among tourists.

In summary, the East Coast of Zanzibar is a paradise for nature lovers, beachgoers, water sports enthusiasts, and those interested in cultural exploration. With its stunning beaches, rich marine life, and opportunities to engage with the local culture, this region offers a well-rounded and memorable experience for travelers.

- South Coast

The South Coast of Zanzibar is a stunning and idyllic region located on the southern tip of the main Unguja Island, which is part of the Zanzibar Archipelago in Tanzania. This area is known for its pristine white sandy beaches, crystal-clear turquoise waters, and a relaxed atmosphere that makes it a popular destination for travelers seeking a tropical paradise. Here, we'll explore some of the key attractions and features of the South Coast in Zanzibar:

1. Beaches: The South Coast boasts some of the most beautiful beaches in the world. The soft, powdery sand and warm waters make it an ideal destination for sunbathing, swimming, and water sports. Popular beaches like Bwejuu Beach and Paje Beach offer a tranquil environment, perfect for relaxation.

2. Marine Life: Zanzibar, and particularly the South Coast, is renowned for its diverse marine life. The region offers fantastic opportunities for snorkeling and diving. You can explore vibrant coral reefs, swim alongside exotic fish, and even spot dolphins or sea turtles.

3. Jozani Chwaka Bay National Park: This national park is located not far from the South Coast and is home to the endemic and endangered Red Colobus Monkey. A visit to this park allows you to observe these unique primates in their natural habitat.

4. Spice Tours: Zanzibar is historically known as the "Spice Island." The South Coast offers various spice

tours where you can discover how spices like cloves, vanilla, and cinnamon are grown and processed.

5. Culture and History: The South Coast is steeped in history and culture. You can explore local villages, interact with the friendly Swahili people, and visit historic sites such as Kizimkazi, which is known for its ancient mosque and stories of the Arab slave trade.

6. Water Sports: The South Coast is a hub for water sports enthusiasts. You can try kiteboarding, windsurfing, and sailing in the strong and consistent winds of this region.

7. Chumbe Island: Just off the South Coast, Chumbe Island Coral Park is a protected marine area and a great place for eco-tourism. It's known for its pristine coral reefs and a unique eco-lodge.

8. Sunset Dhow Cruises: A romantic way to enjoy the breathtaking sunsets of the South Coast is to take a traditional dhow boat cruise. These trips often include local music, fresh seafood, and the opportunity to see the sun dip below the horizon.

9. Accommodations: The South Coast offers a range of accommodations, from luxury beachfront resorts

to more budget-friendly options. Many of these lodgings provide direct access to the beaches and excellent facilities for a comfortable stay.

Overall, the South Coast of Zanzibar is a tropical paradise that offers a mix of natural beauty, cultural experiences, and water-based activities. Whether you're seeking relaxation, adventure, or a combination of both, this region has something to offer for every type of traveler.

- *West Coast*

The West Coast of Zanzibar is a stunning and picturesque region that is renowned for its pristine beaches, vibrant culture, and diverse attractions. Here, I'll provide an overview of what you can expect to experience on the West Coast of Zanzibar:

1. Beaches: The West Coast of Zanzibar is famous for its idyllic beaches with soft, powdery white sand and crystal-clear turquoise waters. Nungwi and Kendwa are some of the most popular beach destinations. Nungwi, in particular, is known for its beautiful sunsets and opportunities for water sports like snorkeling and scuba diving.

2. Nungwi Village: Nungwi, a traditional fishing village turned tourist hub, is located on the

northern tip of the island. It's a vibrant place with a mix of cultures and activities. You can explore the local boatyard, visit the Nungwi Natural Aquarium, or simply relax on the beach.

3. Culture and History: Zanzibar has a rich cultural history, and the West Coast is no exception. You can explore the region's historical sites, including the ruins of Maruhubi Palace and Kidichi Persian Baths. Additionally, the Dhow Countries Music Academy in Stone Town often hosts cultural performances and events.

4. Water Sports: The West Coast offers excellent opportunities for water sports. Snorkelling and diving are popular due to the pristine coral reefs and diverse marine life. Mnemba Atoll, just off the coast, is a famous diving destination.

5. Seafood: Zanzibar, and particularly the West Coast, is known for its delicious seafood. You can enjoy fresh catches of the day at local restaurants and beachfront bars. The sunset views from some of these eateries are truly memorable.

6. Sunset Cruises: Sunset cruises on traditional dhows are a fantastic way to end your day on the West Coast. These leisurely boat rides often include

a stop for snorkeling and provide breathtaking views of the coastline during the golden hour.

7. Mangroves: The western coastline is home to extensive mangrove forests, which can be explored on guided boat tours. These tours offer insight into the local ecosystem and the opportunity to spot various bird species.

8. Luxury Resorts: Zanzibar's West Coast boasts a range of luxury resorts and boutique accommodations that cater to travelers seeking a more opulent experience. Many of these resorts are situated right on the beach and offer all-inclusive packages.

9. Local Markets: Visit the bustling markets in Stone Town and Nungwi to shop for traditional African crafts, spices, and other souvenirs. Haggle with local vendors for unique treasures.

10. Spice Tours: While the primary spice-growing region is in the interior of Zanzibar, you can still explore spice farms and learn about the island's spice production through guided tours.

The West Coast of Zanzibar offers a mix of relaxation, cultural exploration, and adventure.

Whether you're looking to unwind on pristine beaches, delve into the island's history and culture, or partake in water activities, this region has something to offer every type of traveler.

Chapter 4. Accommodation

- *Luxury Resorts*

Zanzibar is a paradise island destination known for its stunning beaches, rich cultural heritage, and vibrant marine life. If you're looking for a luxury resort experience in Zanzibar, there are several exceptional options to consider. Here are some suggestions:

1. Baraza Resort and Spa: This is a top-rated luxury resort located on Bwejuu-Paje Beach. It's known for its exquisite Swahili and Arabian architecture, as well as its all-inclusive packages that include fine dining, spa treatments, and water sports. The resort offers beautiful villas with private plunge pools and direct beach access.

2. Mnemba Island Lodge: If you're seeking exclusivity, Mnemba Island Lodge is an ideal choice. It's a private island resort offering just 10 beachfront bandas. The resort is known for its incredible diving and snorkeling opportunities, and it's an excellent place to experience the untouched beauty of Zanzibar.

3. The Residence Zanzibar: Located in a lush forest along a pristine beach in Kizimkazi, The Residence

Zanzibar offers luxurious villas with private pools and butler service. It's a serene and romantic option for those looking to unwind.

4. Zuri Zanzibar: Nestled on Kendwa Beach, Zuri Zanzibar is a stylish and eco-friendly luxury resort. The resort is known for its infinity pool with a stunning ocean view, contemporary design, and a tranquil atmosphere.

5. Kilindi Zanzibar: This unique resort offers a collection of Pavilion suites, each with its private plunge pool and tropical gardens. The design is minimalist and elegant, providing a sense of tranquillity and seclusion.

6. Park Hyatt Zanzibar: If you prefer staying in Stone Town, the Park Hyatt offers a luxury experience in the heart of the historic city. The hotel combines modern amenities with traditional Zanzibar culture.

7. Essque Zalu Zanzibar: Located in Nungwi, this luxury resort features spacious suites and villas with a unique blend of contemporary design and Swahili-inspired decor. It offers various dining options and a beautiful oceanfront setting.

8. Tulia Zanzibar Unique Beach Resort: Situated in Pongwe, Tulia Zanzibar offers an all-inclusive experience with stylish villas, a spa, and excellent dining. It's known for its attention to detail and personalized service.

9. Matemwe Retreat: For a serene and exclusive getaway, Matemwe Retreat is a great choice. It offers just four villas with private plunge pools, making it perfect for honeymooners or those seeking seclusion.

10. Meliá Zanzibar: This resort is located on the northeast coast of Zanzibar and boasts luxurious rooms and excellent facilities, including an 18-hole golf course. It's a great option for those who want a blend of beachfront relaxation and active pursuits.

When choosing a luxury resort in Zanzibar, consider your preferences, whether it's beachfront, cultural experiences, or seclusion. Zanzibar offers a diverse range of options to cater to various tastes, and you're sure to find a resort that aligns with your idea of a perfect luxury vacation in this tropical paradise. Make sure to check the latest reviews and availability, as the offerings and quality of resorts can change over time.

- *Mid-Range Hotels*

Here are some suggestions for mid-range hotels in Zanzibar:

1. Mizingani Seafront Hotel: Located in Stone Town, this mid-range hotel offers a fantastic view of the Indian Ocean. The hotel combines traditional Zanzibari architecture with modern amenities. It's a great base for exploring the historical attractions of Stone Town.

2. Cristal Resort and Spa: Situated on the picturesque Paje Beach, this mid-range resort provides a relaxed atmosphere. It's an excellent choice for beach lovers. The resort offers various water sports and activities.

3. Maru Maru Hotel: Another Stone Town gem, Maru Maru Hotel is known for its rooftop terrace, which provides panoramic views of the city and ocean. The hotel features a fusion of Swahili and Arabic architectural styles.

4. Zanzibar Palace Hotel: Tucked away in a quiet corner of Stone Town, this boutique hotel offers an intimate experience. Each room is uniquely decorated, reflecting the island's rich history and culture.

5. Warere Beach Hotel: This beachfront property in Nungwi is perfect for those looking to unwind. It's a great choice for couples and honeymooners. The hotel has a tranquil garden, a swimming pool, and easy access to the beach.

6. Fumba Beach Lodge: For a more secluded experience, Fumba Beach Lodge, set on the southwest coast, offers spacious bungalows and privacy. It's ideal for those seeking a peaceful retreat.

7. Sunset Kendwa: Located in Kendwa, this hotel offers affordability without compromising on comfort. Its proximity to Kendwa Rocks, where beach parties are common, is a big draw for younger travellers.

8. Smiles Beach Hotel: Situated in the village of Nungwi, this hotel provides a beachfront location with easy access to water activities. The rooms are well-maintained and comfortable.

9. Zanzibar Coffee House: A unique option in Stone Town, this hotel is known for its strong connection to Zanzibar's coffee culture. It's a cozy and intimate choice, perfect for coffee enthusiasts.

10. Al-Minar Hotel: Another budget-friendly hotel in Stone Town, Al-Minar offers a convenient location and clean, comfortable rooms. It's a good option for travelers looking to explore the town's attractions.

When booking a mid-range hotel in Zanzibar, consider your preferences, such as beachfront access, historical sites, or unique cultural experiences. Additionally, check for reviews, amenities, and package deals to make the most of your stay on this beautiful island. Keep in mind that Zanzibar's popularity as a tourist destination means that prices can fluctuate, so booking in advance is advisable.

- Budget Lodging

Budget lodging in Zanzibar can be a great way to enjoy this beautiful island without breaking the bank. Here are some suggestions for budget travelers:

1. Hostels and Guesthouses: Zanzibar offers a variety of hostels and guesthouses, particularly in Stone Town, where you can find budget accommodation options. These often provide dormitory-style rooms, making it affordable for solo

travelers or those on a tight budget. Some popular choices include Lost & Found Hostel and Jambo Brothers Hostel.

2. Home Stays: Staying with a local family can be an excellent way to experience Zanzibar's culture and save money. Many locals open up their homes to tourists, offering a more authentic and affordable stay.

3. Online Booking: Use online booking platforms like Booking.com, Hostelworld, or Airbnb to find affordable accommodation options. These platforms often offer a range of budget choices, and you can read reviews from other travelers to ensure quality.

4. Off-Peak Travel: Consider visiting Zanzibar during the off-peak season, typically from March to May and November to mid-December. Accommodation prices are lower, and you'll encounter fewer crowds.

5. Beach Bungalows: If you're looking for an affordable beach experience, you can find beachfront bungalows and cottages at a fraction of the cost of luxury resorts. Paje and Nungwi are great places to find such options.

6. Backpacker's Resorts: Some resorts cater to budget travelers with backpacker-friendly facilities, such as shared kitchen areas and communal spaces. These can provide a more relaxed and social atmosphere while keeping costs down.

7. Local Food: Look for lodging options close to local markets and restaurants. By eating at local food stalls and small eateries, you can save a significant amount on your daily food expenses.

8. Negotiate: Don't hesitate to negotiate prices, especially if you're planning a longer stay. Many places in Zanzibar are open to negotiation, and you might get a better deal.

9. Use Local Transportation: Zanzibar is a relatively small island, and you can explore it using the local dala-dala minibuses or rent a bicycle. This will save you money on transportation and allow you to experience the local way of life.

10. Book in Advance: If you know your travel dates in advance, booking your accommodation early can often lead to discounts and better deals.

11. Island Hopping: Instead of staying in one place, consider exploring multiple areas on the island. This can give you a chance to experience different parts of Zanzibar and may lead to more affordable lodging options.

12. Travel with a Group: If you're traveling with friends or family, consider renting a private villa or apartment. Splitting the cost among a group can make this a budget-friendly option.

Remember to check the latest reviews and ratings for accommodations, as quality can vary. With some planning and research, you can enjoy your Zanzibar trip on a budget while still savouring the island's unique charm and beauty.

- Unique Stays

Zanzibar, a semi-autonomous archipelago off the coast of Tanzania, is a destination known for its stunning beaches, rich history, and vibrant culture. When it comes to accommodation, there are plenty of unique and memorable options to choose from. Here are some suggestions for unique stays in Zanzibar:

1. Overwater Bungalows: Zanzibar offers some luxurious overwater bungalows that provide an

unmatched experience. These accommodations often come with direct access to the crystal-clear waters, offering breathtaking views of the Indian Ocean. Resorts like the Zanzibar White Sand Luxury Villas & Spa provide these unique bungalows.

2. Historical Stone Town Hotels: Zanzibar's Stone Town is a UNESCO World Heritage site and a place where you can immerse yourself in the island's history. Staying in a historic hotel like Emerson Spice or Jafferji House and Spa allows you to experience the charm of old Zanzibar while enjoying modern comforts.

3. Treehouse Lodges: For a more adventurous and unique experience, consider staying in a treehouse lodge. Places like Chumbe Island Coral Park offer eco-friendly treehouses that are tucked away in lush greenery, providing both seclusion and tranquility.

4. Private Villas: Many private villas and vacation rentals are available on the island. These are perfect for those seeking privacy and the feeling of a home away from home. You can find villas with private pools and direct beach access for an exclusive experience.

5. Beachfront Glamping: Zanzibar offers the opportunity to enjoy glamping on its beautiful beaches. Some accommodations provide luxurious tented camps right on the beach, where you can fall asleep to the sound of the waves and wake up to stunning sunrises.

6. Sailing and Liveaboard Experiences: Explore the archipelago from a different perspective by staying on a sailing boat or yacht. Some operators offer liveaboard experiences that combine diving and sailing, allowing you to discover the marine beauty of Zanzibar.

7. Secluded Beach Huts: There are hidden gems like Mchanga Beach Lodge that offer rustic beach huts set on secluded shores. These simple yet charming huts provide an authentic, off-the-grid experience.

8. Cave Hotels: In Zanzibar's north coast, there are unique cave hotels like The Rock, which are perched on a large coral rock in the ocean. You can enjoy a meal with panoramic sea views or stay in one of their unique rooms.

9. Boutique Hotels: Zanzibar boasts several boutique hotels that offer a personalized and intimate experience. Places like Matemwe Lodge or

Kilindi Zanzibar focus on attention to detail and exclusivity.

10. Spice Plantation Lodges: Zanzibar is renowned for its spices. Consider staying at a spice plantation lodge, such as the Kichanga Lodge, where you can immerse yourself in the scents and flavors of the island.

When booking a unique stay in Zanzibar, it's essential to plan in advance, especially during peak tourist seasons. Also, keep in mind the location that suits your interests, whether it's the vibrant culture of Stone Town, the tranquility of the northern beaches, or the adventurous south coast. Zanzibar offers a diverse range of accommodations that cater to various tastes, making it an unforgettable destination for any traveler.

Chapter 5. Things to Do

- *Exploring Stone Town*

Exploring Stone Town in Zanzibar is an enchanting experience that takes you back in time to the island's rich history and culture. Stone Town, the historic heart of Zanzibar City, is a UNESCO World Heritage Site, known for its unique architecture, narrow winding streets, and vibrant atmosphere. Here's a guide to exploring this captivating destination:

1. Historical Significance:
   - Stone Town served as the capital of the Sultanate of Zanzibar in the 19th century. Its history is intertwined with the East African slave trade, as well as the spice and ivory trades.
   - The architecture of Stone Town reflects a blend of Swahili, Arab, Persian, Indian, and European influences, showcasing its diverse past.

2. Architecture:
   - One of the most remarkable aspects of Stone Town is its architecture. The buildings are made of coral stone, giving the town its name. Ornate wooden doors, carved balconies, and intricate designs are common features.

3. Attractions:

   - The Old Fort (Ngome Kongwe): A 17th-century fort built by the Portuguese and later used by the Omani Arabs. It now hosts events and cultural performances.

   - House of Wonders (Beit al Ajaib): This grand palace is a symbol of Zanzibar's rich history and is a must-visit museum.

   - Forodhani Gardens: This waterfront area is famous for its vibrant night market where you can sample a variety of local dishes.

   - Sultan's Palace (Beit el-Sahel): The former residence of the Sultan of Zanzibar, now a museum showcasing royal artefacts.

   - Old Dispensary (Ithnashiri Dispensary): A stunning building known for its intricate architecture.

   - Christ Church Cathedral: A stunning Anglican cathedral with a mix of Gothic and Moorish architectural elements.

   - Mercury House: The birthplace of Queen frontman Freddie Mercury, now a popular tourist attraction.

4. Markets and Shopping:

   - Stone Town offers fantastic shopping opportunities. Visit the Darajani Market for fresh produce, spices, and local crafts. You can also explore local shops for unique souvenirs.

5. Culture and Food:
   - Stone Town is a cultural melting pot, and you'll find a mix of Swahili, Arab, and Indian influences in its cuisine. Don't miss trying Zanzibar's famous dishes like biryani, pilau, and fresh seafood.
   - The town is also home to various cultural festivals, including the Zanzibar International Film Festival (ZIFF), which celebrates the arts and culture of the region.

6. Spice Tours:
   - Zanzibar is renowned for its spices, and Stone Town is an excellent starting point for spice tours that take you to the island's lush spice plantations.

7. Beaches:
   - While Stone Town itself is not known for its beaches, you can easily access nearby pristine beaches on the island's east and north coasts. These make for great day trips or longer excursions.

8. Accommodation:
   - Stone Town offers a range of accommodations, from luxury boutique hotels to budget-friendly

guesthouses, many of which are set in historic buildings.

Exploring Stone Town is a journey through history, culture, and the diverse heritage of Zanzibar. It's a destination that captivates travelers with its unique atmosphere and the timeless charm of its narrow alleyways and historic buildings. Whether you're interested in history, architecture, culture, or simply enjoying the vibrant local life, Stone Town has something for everyone.

- *Beach Activities*

Beach activities in Zanzibar are a delightful blend of natural beauty, cultural experiences, and water-based adventures. Zanzibar, an archipelago off the coast of Tanzania in East Africa, is renowned for its pristine, white sandy beaches, crystal-clear waters, and a rich cultural heritage. Here's an overview of the beach activities you can enjoy in this exotic destination:

1. Swimming and Sunbathing: Zanzibar boasts some of the most beautiful beaches in the world, such as Nungwi, Kendwa, and Paje. These beaches offer ideal conditions for swimming and sunbathing. The warm, turquoise waters are perfect

for a relaxing dip, and the soft sand is inviting for sun worshippers.

2. Snorkeling and Diving: The surrounding coral reefs are a haven for underwater enthusiasts. You can explore a mesmerizing world of marine life, including colorful corals, tropical fish, and even the chance to spot larger species like dolphins and sea turtles. Mnemba Atoll is a famous diving spot, while Chumbe Island Coral Park is a marine conservation area that offers guided snorkeling tours.

3. KiteSurfing and WindSurfing: Paje Beach is a hub for kite surfing and wind surfing. The consistent trade winds make this location perfect for these exhilarating water sports. You can take lessons if you're a beginner or rent equipment if you're experienced.

4. Sailing and Dhow Cruises: Traditional wooden dhows dot the coastline, and you can embark on a dhow cruise to explore the islands and enjoy stunning sunsets. Sunset dhow cruises are particularly popular and romantic.

5. Fishing: Zanzibar has a rich fishing culture, and you can go on fishing expeditions to catch game fish

like marlins, tuna, and sailfish. Many tour operators offer deep-sea fishing trips.

6. Beach Volleyball and Soccer: Some beach resorts offer sports facilities, and you can engage in beach volleyball or soccer with fellow travelers or locals. It's a fun way to stay active while enjoying the scenic beauty of the beaches.

7. Spa and Wellness: After a day of activities, unwind with a spa treatment on the beach. Many resorts and beachfront properties offer a range of relaxation and wellness options, from massages to yoga sessions.

8. Cultural Experiences: Zanzibar is also known for its rich Swahili culture. You can explore nearby villages, visit spice farms, and enjoy local music and dance performances. Don't miss Stone Town, a UNESCO World Heritage site, where you can explore historic buildings, markets, and learn about the island's history.

9. Island Hopping: Zanzibar is not just one island but a collection of them. You can take boat trips to visit nearby islands like Prison Island, Chumbe Island, and Mnemba Island, each with its own unique charm and attractions.

10. Seafood Dining: Zanzibar's coastal location means an abundance of seafood. Enjoy fresh catches of the day at beachfront restaurants while taking in stunning ocean views.

Remember that Zanzibar is a tropical paradise with a tropical climate, so it's important to plan your activities around the weather and seasons. Whether you're seeking relaxation, adventure, or a mix of both, the beach activities in Zanzibar offer something for every type of traveler in a breathtaking and culturally rich setting.

- Spice Tours

Spice tours in Zanzibar offer visitors a unique opportunity to explore the vibrant history, culture, and agriculture of this stunning island in the Indian Ocean. Zanzibar, often referred to as the "Spice Island," is renowned for its rich history in the spice trade. The island's spice tours are a popular attraction, providing an immersive experience into the cultivation, harvesting, and uses of various spices that have been a cornerstone of Zanzibar's economy for centuries.

1. History and Significance:

Zanzibar's spice industry has deep historical roots. The island was a major hub for the spice trade, especially cloves, during the 19th century. These spices played a pivotal role in the island's history, attracting traders and colonizers from various parts of the world. The spice tours allow visitors to connect with this history and understand the importance of spices in shaping the island's culture and economy.

2. Spice Plantations:

Spice tours typically include visits to local plantations where spices like cloves, vanilla, nutmeg, cinnamon, and black pepper are cultivated. You'll have the opportunity to see how these spices are grown, harvested, and processed. Knowledgeable guides provide insights into the cultivation techniques and the specific conditions required for each spice to thrive.

3. Cultural Immersion:

Beyond just the spices, these tours also offer a glimpse into the vibrant culture of Zanzibar. You may witness traditional Swahili farming methods and interact with local farmers. It's an excellent opportunity to learn about the traditional and sustainable practices that have been passed down through generations.

4. Sensory Experience:
   One of the highlights of spice tours is the sensory experience. You can touch, smell, and even taste the spices right from the source. It's a sensory journey that immerses you in the world of flavours and aromas, giving you a deeper appreciation for these culinary essentials.

5. Cooking Demonstrations:
   Many spice tours include cooking demonstrations where you can see how these spices are used in traditional Zanzibar dishes. This provides a hands-on experience, and you can even participate in preparing a meal using freshly picked spices.

6. Scenic Landscapes:
   Zanzibar's spice plantations are often set in picturesque landscapes, featuring lush greenery, tropical gardens, and serene surroundings. The tours not only offer an educational experience but also a chance to appreciate the island's natural beauty.

7. Cultural and Ecological Sustainability:
   These tours often emphasize sustainable agriculture and ecological practices, shedding light on the importance of preserving these resources.

Visitors can gain insights into how local communities and initiatives are working to maintain a balance between agriculture and environmental conservation.

8. Local Artisan Crafts:
Some spice tours also include visits to local markets or workshops where you can purchase spice-related products such as essential oils, perfumes, soaps, and artisan crafts made from spices. This provides an opportunity to support local businesses and take home unique souvenirs.

9. Accessibility:
Spice tours are accessible to a wide range of visitors, from solo travelers to families, and are often suitable for all ages. The gentle nature of the tours makes them a popular choice for tourists looking for a relaxed and educational outing.

Conclusion:
Spice tours in Zanzibar offer a holistic experience, blending history, culture, and the natural environment. They provide an opportunity to appreciate the island's rich heritage while enjoying a sensory journey through the world of spices. Whether you're a food enthusiast, a history buff, or a nature lover, Zanzibar's spice tours have

something to offer to all types of travelers, making them an essential part of any visit to this enchanting island.

- *Water Sports*

Water sports in Zanzibar are a popular and exciting way to explore the stunning coastline and crystal-clear waters of this Indian Ocean paradise. Zanzibar, a semi-autonomous archipelago off the coast of Tanzania, is renowned for its pristine beaches, warm tropical climate, and a wide range of water activities. Here's an overview of the water sports you can enjoy in Zanzibar:

1. Snorkelling: Zanzibar boasts some of the best snorkelling spots in the world. The coral reefs surrounding the islands are teeming with colourful marine life. Mnemba Atoll, located off the northeastern coast, is a particularly famous snorkelling destination.

2. Scuba Diving: For those looking to explore the underwater world in more depth, scuba diving is a must. PADI-certified dive centers are scattered around Zanzibar, offering courses for beginners and guided dives for experienced divers. You can encounter a variety of marine creatures, including

turtles, dolphins, and even the occasional whale shark.

3. Kite Surfing: Zanzibar's consistent trade winds and shallow waters make it an ideal destination for kitesurfing. Paje on the east coast is known for its kite surfing schools and rental shops, catering to both beginners and advanced riders.

4. Windsurfing: Similar to kite surfing, windsurfing is a popular water sport in Zanzibar. The warm waters and steady winds provide excellent conditions for windsurfers of all levels.

5. Stand-Up Paddleboarding (SUP): Paddleboarding is a peaceful way to explore the coastline, lagoons, and mangrove forests of Zanzibar. You can rent paddleboards at various beachfront locations.

6. Kayaking: Kayaking is a relaxing way to explore Zanzibar's coastline and mangrove forests. Many tour operators offer guided kayaking trips, allowing you to experience the natural beauty and wildlife up close.

7. Deep Sea Fishing: Zanzibar is a renowned destination for deep-sea fishing. The waters are rich

in game fish such as marlin, sailfish, and tuna. Many fishing charters operate on the island, catering to both beginners and experienced anglers.

8. Boat Tours: Take a traditional dhow cruise to experience the island from a different perspective. Sunset cruises and day trips to nearby islands like Prison Island and Chumbe Island are popular options.

9. Swimming with Dolphins: Zanzibar offers opportunities to swim with dolphins in their natural habitat. The southern coast, particularly Kizimkazi, is famous for dolphin-watching tours and snorkelling excursions with these graceful creatures.

10. Jet Skiing: Jet skiing is available at various beach resorts, providing an adrenaline rush on the turquoise waters of Zanzibar.

11. Parasailing: For those seeking an exhilarating adventure, parasailing is an option. You can soar above the ocean and enjoy breathtaking views of the coastline.

12. Island Hopping: Zanzibar is surrounded by smaller islands, each with its own unique charm.

You can take boat trips to explore islands like Changuu (Prison Island), Nakupenda, and Mnemba, which offer pristine beaches and rich marine life.

In conclusion, Zanzibar's stunning natural beauty and favorable climate make it a water sports paradise. Whether you're a beginner looking for a leisurely experience or an adrenaline junkie seeking thrills, the archipelago has something to offer to water sports enthusiasts of all levels. Be sure to check the weather and wind conditions to plan your activities accordingly, and respect the local marine ecosystems to ensure that Zanzibar remains an idyllic destination for water sports enthusiasts for years to come.

- *Jozani Forest*

Jozani Forest, located in Zanzibar, Tanzania, is a unique and ecologically significant natural reserve that offers a diverse range of flora and fauna, as well as cultural and historical significance. Here is an overview of Jozani Forest:

1. Location and Geography:
   Jozani Forest is situated in the central-eastern region of Zanzibar, an island located off the coast of Tanzania. It covers an area of approximately 50

square kilometers (19 square miles) and is a vital part of Zanzibar's natural landscape.

2. Biodiversity:
   One of the primary attractions of Jozani Forest is its rich biodiversity. The forest is home to a variety of plant and animal species, some of which are endemic to the region. The most famous inhabitants of the forest are the rare and endangered Zanzibar red colobus monkey (Procolobus kirkii), which can only be found on this island. The forest also shelters other primates like Sykes' monkeys, as well as various bird species, reptiles, and insects.

3. Conservation Efforts:
   Jozani Forest has been recognized for its importance in conserving the red colobus monkey and its habitat. Efforts have been made to protect and preserve the forest and its inhabitants. Conservation organisations, in collaboration with the government of Zanzibar, have implemented various initiatives to ensure the survival of these endangered species.

4. Ecological Significance:
   The forest acts as a crucial ecosystem for the island, contributing to soil conservation, water

purification, and providing habitat for various species. It also plays a role in supporting Zanzibar's unique and diverse flora.

5. Mangroves:
   Part of Jozani Forest consists of mangrove forests that are ecologically important in coastal regions. These mangroves provide a habitat for marine life and help protect the coastline from erosion. They also serve as a nursery for various fish and crustacean species.

6. Visitor Experience:
   Jozani Forest is open to tourists and offers guided tours. Visitors can explore the forest, observe the wildlife, and learn about the ecology and conservation efforts. The iconic red colobus monkeys are often the highlight of these tours.

7. Cultural and Historical Significance:
   Jozani Forest is not only a natural wonder but also holds cultural and historical importance. The forest is believed to be sacred by the local communities and is intertwined with their traditions and folklore.

8. Challenges:

Despite conservation efforts, Jozani Forest faces challenges such as habitat loss due to deforestation, agricultural expansion, and the impact of tourism. These issues require ongoing attention to balance conservation with the needs of the local population.

In summary, Jozani Forest in Zanzibar is a remarkable natural reserve that is home to unique and endangered species, particularly the Zanzibar red colobus monkey. It serves as a vital hub for biodiversity and ecological balance, while also playing a role in the cultural and historical tapestry of Zanzibar. Conservation efforts are crucial to ensure its continued survival and to protect the natural heritage of the region.

- Historical Sites

Zanzibar, an archipelago off the coast of Tanzania in East Africa, is a region with a rich history that is reflected in its numerous historical sites. Here, I will provide an overview of some of the most notable historical sites on the main island of Unguja (commonly referred to as Zanzibar) and the smaller island of Pemba.

1. Stone Town:
   Stone Town is the historical heart of Zanzibar and a UNESCO World Heritage Site. It is known for its

labyrinthine streets, intricate architecture, and historical significance. The town was a major hub for the spice and slave trades, and its buildings display a blend of Swahili, Arab, Persian, and European architectural influences. Some prominent attractions in Stone Town include the Old Fort, the House of Wonders, the Arab Fort, and the Forodhani Gardens.

2. Palace Museum (Beit al-Sahel):

The Palace Museum, also known as Beit al-Sahel, was once the Sultan's palace. Today, it serves as a museum that showcases Zanzibar's royal history. Visitors can explore the Sultan's living quarters, royal carriages, and various artifacts from the island's past.

3. Old Slave Market Site:

Zanzibar played a significant role in the trans-Indian Ocean slave trade, and the Old Slave Market Site is a haunting reminder of this dark history. Visitors can see the underground chambers where slaves were held before being sold, as well as the Anglican Cathedral built on the site after the abolition of slavery.

4. Jozani Chwaka Bay National Park:

While not a historical site in the traditional sense, this national park on Zanzibar is a vital location for conservation and ecotourism. It is home to the Zanzibar red colobus monkey, an endangered primate species found only on the island.

5. Maruhubi Palace Ruins:
    The Maruhubi Palace was once a grand residence of the Sultan's family. Today, it lies in ruins but provides a glimpse into Zanzibar's aristocratic past. Visitors can explore the site and learn about its history.

6. Mangapwani Slave Chamber:
    Located on the northern coast of Zanzibar, the Mangapwani Slave Chamber is another grim reminder of the island's role in the slave trade. It was a place where slaves were hidden before being transported. Visitors can explore the chambers and learn about this tragic period in Zanzibar's history.

7. Kidichi Persian Baths:
    The Kidichi Persian Baths are an interesting historical site that reflects the Persian influence on Zanzibar. These baths were built in the 19th century for the wife of Sultan Barghash. They are a fascinating blend of Persian and Swahili architectural styles.

8. Hamamni Persian Baths:
   Another set of Persian baths on the island, the Hamamni Persian Baths, were used for relaxation and personal hygiene. They offer a unique look at Zanzibar's diverse cultural influences.

These historical sites in Zanzibar offer a window into the island's complex and multifaceted history, including its role in the spice and slave trades, the influence of various cultures, and the legacy of its sultans. Exploring these sites not only provides a deeper understanding of Zanzibar's past but also offers a unique travel experience in a place with a rich and storied history.

- Cultural Experiences

Zanzibar, an archipelago off the coast of Tanzania in East Africa, is a place of rich cultural diversity and unique experiences. The cultural tapestry of Zanzibar is a blend of African, Arab, Indian, and European influences, making it a captivating destination for those seeking a deep immersion into a different way of life. Here's an overview of the cultural experiences you can encounter in Zanzibar:

1. Swahili Culture: The predominant culture in Zanzibar is Swahili, and the Swahili language is

widely spoken. The culture is characterised by its fusion of African, Arab, and Indian elements, reflected in the architecture, cuisine, and traditional clothing. Visitors can learn about the Swahili way of life by interacting with locals, visiting markets, and participating in cultural events.

2. Stone Town: The capital city of Zanzibar, Stone Town, is a UNESCO World Heritage Site renowned for its historic architecture and narrow winding streets. The city's buildings feature intricate wooden doors and balconies, which showcase Arab and Indian architectural influences. Exploring Stone Town is like stepping back in time.

3. Spice Tours: Zanzibar is often referred to as the "Spice Island" due to its historic role as a major spice producer. You can take guided tours of spice plantations to learn about the cultivation and processing of spices like cloves, vanilla, nutmeg, and cinnamon. It's a sensory experience that provides insights into the island's agricultural heritage.

4. Dhow Cruises: Traditional sailing vessels called dhows are an integral part of Zanzibar culture. Taking a dhow cruise along the crystal-clear waters of the Indian Ocean is a popular activity. These

cruises offer breathtaking views of the coastline, opportunities for snorkeling, and an authentic cultural experience, often accompanied by live music and delicious seafood.

5. Local Cuisine: Zanzibar's cuisine is a delicious reflection of its cultural diversity. Dishes like biryani, pilau, and samosas showcase Indian and Arab influences, while fresh seafood is a staple. You can savor these flavors at local restaurants or try your hand at cooking during a Swahili cooking class.

6. Cultural Festivals: Zanzibar hosts several cultural festivals throughout the year. The Zanzibar International Film Festival (ZIFF) and Sauti za Busara music festival are notable events that celebrate art, film, and music from Africa and beyond. These festivals offer a unique opportunity to engage with local and international artists and cultural enthusiasts.

7. Historical Sites: Zanzibar has a rich historical past, including its role in the transatlantic slave trade. You can visit historical sites like the Old Slave Market, the Sultan's Palace Museum, and the Anglican Cathedral to learn about this history and its impact on the island.

8. Traditional Clothing and Art: Zanzibari women often wear vibrant and colorful kangas and kikois, which are traditional garments. You can purchase these clothing items and other local handicrafts in the markets. Additionally, Zanzibar is known for its intricate henna art, which is often displayed on the hands and feet of women during cultural celebrations.

9. Local Music and Dance: Taarab music, influenced by Arabic, Indian, and African rhythms, is a key part of Zanzibar culture. You can enjoy live Taarab performances and even participate in traditional dance performances, where locals often welcome visitors to join in the fun.

10. Religious Diversity: Zanzibar is home to a mix of religious beliefs, with Islam being the predominant religion. Visitors can witness the call to prayer, explore mosques, and engage in respectful conversations about religious customs and practices.

In conclusion, Zanzibar offers a plethora of cultural experiences that provide a unique window into the island's rich and diverse heritage. Whether you're wandering the ancient streets of Stone Town, savoring flavorful dishes, or participating in local festivities, you'll find a vibrant tapestry of cultures waiting to be explored on this enchanting island.

Chapter 6. Dining and Cuisine

- *Zanzibari Food*

Zanzibari food is a unique and diverse cuisine that reflects the island's rich history and cultural influences. Zanzibar, an archipelago off the coast of Tanzania, has been a historical hub for traders and travelers from around the world, and this has greatly influenced its culinary traditions. Here, I'll provide an overview of Zanzibari food:

1. Historical and Cultural Influences:
   Zanzibar's food culture has been shaped by centuries of trade and colonization. Arab, Indian, Persian, Portuguese, and African influences have all left their mark on Zanzibari cuisine. The island's history as a major spice trade center also plays a crucial role in the development of its flavors.

2. Spices:
   Zanzibar is often referred to as the "Spice Island" due to its production of spices like cloves, cinnamon, cardamom, and nutmeg. These spices are integral to many Zanzibari dishes, adding depth and aroma to the cuisine.

3. Staple Ingredients:

- Rice: Rice is a staple food in Zanzibar and is often served with a variety of curries and stews.

- Seafood: Given its coastal location, seafood plays a prominent role. You can find dishes featuring fish, octopus, lobster, and crab.

- Coconut: Coconut milk and grated coconut are commonly used to add creaminess and flavour to dishes.

- Plantains and Cassava: These starchy vegetables are essential components of many meals.

- Chilies: Zanzibari cuisine is known for its spiciness, with chilies frequently used to add heat to dishes.

4. Popular Dishes:

- Biryani: Zanzibari biryani is a fragrant and flavorful rice dish often made with marinated meat or seafood.

- Urojo: This is a spicy soup made with a mix of ingredients including lentils, potatoes, and various spices.

- Pilau: Zanzibari pilau is a spiced rice dish often cooked with meat, vegetables, and a blend of aromatic spices.

- Zanzibar Pizza (Pizza Maandazi): This is a popular street food, which is more like a savory, stuffed pastry with various fillings.

- Mishkaki: Skewered and grilled meat, similar to kebabs, often marinated in flavorful spices.

5. Street Food Culture:
Zanzibar has a vibrant street food culture. Local vendors sell dishes like Zanzibar pizza, seafood skewers, and a variety of snacks and sweets along the streets, especially in Stone Town, the capital.

6. Sweets and Desserts:
Zanzibari sweets often feature coconut, cardamom, and sugar. You can find dishes like kashata (coconut and sugar sweets), mkate wa sinia (a type of flatbread), and mahamri (sweet fried dough).

7. Beverages:
- Spiced Tea (Chai ya Tangawizi): Zanzibari tea is known for its use of spices like ginger, cloves, and cardamom.
- Coconut Water: Fresh coconut water is widely available and a refreshing drink in the tropical climate.

8. Eating Etiquette:
It's common to eat with your hands, especially for traditional dishes. However, utensils are also available in most restaurants. Sharing food is a

common practice, reflecting the island's communal culture.

9. Food Festivals:
   Zanzibar hosts various food festivals throughout the year, celebrating its diverse cuisine. The Zanzibar Food Festival is one such event where visitors can taste a wide array of dishes.

In conclusion, Zanzibari food is a delightful fusion of flavors and cultures. The island's historical influences, abundant spices, and coastal location have given rise to a unique and diverse culinary tradition that continues to captivate visitors with its aromatic and flavorful dishes.

- Restaurants and Cafes

Zanzibar, a picturesque island off the coast of Tanzania in East Africa, is known for its stunning beaches, rich history, and vibrant culture. It's also a place where you can savor a diverse array of culinary delights at its restaurants and cafes. Let's explore the restaurant and cafe scene in Zanzibar:

1. Seafood Delights:
   Zanzibar is renowned for its seafood, and you can find a plethora of restaurants specializing in freshly caught fish, lobster, and prawns. The Forodhani

Gardens in Stone Town come alive in the evening with an array of street food vendors offering a variety of seafood dishes, including grilled octopus and Zanzibar pizza.

2. Swahili Cuisine:
   Swahili cuisine is at the heart of Zanzibar's culinary scene. It's a fusion of African, Indian, Arab, and Persian influences, resulting in dishes rich in flavor. Many restaurants serve traditional Swahili fare like biryani, pilau, and the famous Zanzibar mix, a platter of different curries and condiments.

3. Spice Plantations:
   Zanzibar is often called the "Spice Island" due to its extensive spice plantations. Some restaurants offer tours that include spice tastings and elaborate traditional Swahili meals. You can learn about the cultivation of spices like cloves, cinnamon, and nutmeg while enjoying a unique dining experience.

4. Fine Dining:
   For those seeking a more upscale dining experience, Zanzibar boasts high-end restaurants with stunning oceanfront views. These establishments often serve a mix of international and fusion cuisine, combining the island's fresh ingredients with global culinary influences.

5. Cafes and Coffee:

Zanzibar is also home to charming cafes where you can enjoy a leisurely cup of locally grown coffee or a refreshing glass of spiced chai. These cafes often serve homemade pastries and light snacks in a relaxed atmosphere.

6. Sunset Bars:

With its breathtaking sunsets, Zanzibar has numerous bars and cafes along its shoreline where you can sip on cocktails while watching the sun dip below the Indian Ocean. Kendwa and Nungwi beaches are popular spots for this.

7. Cultural Experiences:

Some restaurants offer more than just food; they provide cultural experiences. You may find venues that host live traditional music and dance performances, giving visitors a deeper understanding of the island's rich heritage.

8. Dietary Options:

Zanzibar caters to various dietary preferences, including vegan and vegetarian choices. Many places offer a range of fresh salads, vegetable dishes, and plant-based options.

9. Local Markets:
   Don't forget to explore local markets where you can sample street food and traditional snacks. You'll find everything from samosas and mandazi (doughnuts) to fresh fruit and sugar cane juice.

10. Sustainability:
   Zanzibar is increasingly focused on sustainable and eco-friendly practices, and this extends to its dining scene. Some restaurants and cafes emphasize local sourcing and eco-conscious operations.

In summary, Zanzibar offers a rich tapestry of dining options, from simple street food to upscale dining with an ocean view. Whether you're interested in savoring Swahili flavors, enjoying fresh seafood, or embracing the island's vibrant culture, Zanzibar's restaurants and cafes have something to satisfy every palate.

- Street Food

Street food in Zanzibar is a vibrant and integral part of the local culture and culinary scene. Zanzibar, an archipelago off the coast of Tanzania, boasts a rich history of trade and influences from various cultures, which is reflected in its diverse and delicious street food offerings. Here's an overview of street food in Zanzibar:

1. Mishkaki: These are skewered and grilled pieces of marinated meat, usually beef or chicken. They are often accompanied by a side of tangy, spicy sauces. Mishkaki stalls are common throughout Zanzibar, and the aroma of sizzling meat is hard to resist.

2. Zanzibar Pizza (Mandazi): Zanzibar's version of pizza is quite different from the Italian classic. Zanzibar pizza is a savory or sweet crepe-like snack filled with various ingredients. You can find them with fillings like cheese, minced meat, or even sugar and coconut.

3. Urojo: Urojo is a tangy soup that's a unique specialty in Zanzibar. It's made with a mixture of spices, lentils, and potatoes, and often includes fried or grilled seafood. It's a flavorful and spicy dish that locals and tourists enjoy.

4. Forodhani Gardens: This is a popular gathering spot in Stone Town, Zanzibar's capital, known for its bustling street food stalls. At night, the area comes alive with vendors selling a variety of dishes,

including grilled seafood, samosas, sugar cane juice, and much more.

5. Zanzibar Mix: Zanzibar mix is a must-try street food delight. It's a combination of various snacks like fried cassava, plantains, and potatoes, served with a spicy sauce. The blend of textures and flavors makes it a favorite among locals.

6. Vitumbua: These small, sweet, deep-fried rice cakes are a popular snack or dessert. They are crispy on the outside and soft on the inside, often flavored with coconut or cardamom.

7. Seafood Delights: Zanzibar's coastal location means an abundance of fresh seafood. Street food vendors offer grilled, fried, or stewed fish, prawns, octopus, and lobster. You can savor the catch of the day right by the sea.

8. Sugar Cane Juice: To quench your thirst, try a refreshing glass of freshly squeezed sugar cane juice. It's a popular beverage in Zanzibar and offers a sweet respite from the tropical heat.

9. Biryani: Zanzibar's biryani is a flavorful and aromatic rice dish often served with marinated chicken or beef. The spice blend used in Zanzibari

biryani is unique and reflects the island's cultural diversity.

10. Samosas: Samosas are a global favorite, and in Zanzibar, they are filled with spiced meat or vegetables and fried to golden perfection. They make for a delightful, on-the-go snack.

11. Sugarcane: Zanzibar's sugarcane is famously sweet and delicious. Vendors often sell peeled and sliced sugarcane, making for a refreshing and natural treat.

12. Ukodo: This is a hearty beef soup made with plantains and potatoes. It's a flavorful and filling dish, especially enjoyed during special occasions and gatherings.

13. Mangoes and Pineapples: Zanzibar's tropical climate ensures that the island produces an abundance of sweet, juicy mangoes and pineapples. You can find vendors selling these fruits on many street corners.

14. Street Coffee: Zanzibar is known for its strong and aromatic coffee. Street vendors often brew fresh coffee for you to enjoy, usually served with a hint of spice and sweetness.

In Zanzibar, street food isn't just about satisfying hunger; it's an immersive experience that allows you to explore the island's rich history, culture, and diverse flavors. The fusion of African, Arab, Indian, and European influences in Zanzibar's cuisine makes it a unique and delightful destination for food enthusiasts. So, if you ever find yourself on this beautiful island, don't miss the chance to savor its street food offerings.

Chapter 7. Shopping

- *Local Markets*

Local markets in Zanzibar are vibrant and integral to the island's culture and economy. These markets offer a fascinating glimpse into the unique blend of African, Arab, and Indian influences that define the region. Here, we'll explore the significance, diversity, and charm of local markets in Zanzibar.

1. Economic Significance:
   Local markets play a crucial role in Zanzibar's economy. They serve as hubs for trade and commerce, providing income to countless individuals. These markets often feature a wide variety of goods, including fresh produce, spices, textiles, and handicrafts. Tourists and locals alike flock to these markets, contributing significantly to the local economy.

2. Spices and Agriculture:
   Zanzibar is known as the "Spice Island" for its thriving spice trade. The marketplaces, such as the Darajani Market in Stone Town, offer a rich selection of spices like cloves, cardamom, cinnamon, and vanilla. The vibrant agricultural products include fresh fruits, vegetables, and exotic fruits like jackfruit and rambutan.

3. Handicrafts and Souvenirs:

Local markets are excellent places to purchase unique handicrafts and souvenirs. Skilled artisans create intricate wood carvings, colorful fabrics, and beaded jewelry, all reflecting the island's rich cultural heritage. Visitors can find one-of-a-kind pieces that make for memorable keepsakes.

4. Cultural Diversity:

The markets in Zanzibar are a melting pot of cultures. This is reflected in the products on offer, as well as the diverse group of vendors and shoppers. The island's history of trade and migration has resulted in a fusion of Swahili, Arab, and Indian influences, all of which are evident in the markets' offerings.

5. Social Hubs:

Beyond economic activities, local markets are also social hubs. They are places where people gather, interact, and share stories. It's common to find vendors sharing local anecdotes and travelers engaging in cultural exchanges. Markets offer a sense of community, connecting people from different walks of life.

6. Food Markets:

Zanzibar's food markets are a gastronomic delight. Fresh seafood, including octopus, lobsters, and a variety of fish, are abundant. Local chefs serve up delectable dishes like Zanzibari biryani, grilled mishkaki, and samosas, providing a taste of authentic Swahili cuisine.

7. Traditional Clothing:

Visitors can explore and buy traditional clothing such as kangas and kitenges, which are colorful and widely worn by the locals. These textiles are often used for clothing, but they also make for fantastic fabrics to take back home.

8. Sustainability and Conservation:

Some local markets in Zanzibar are taking steps towards sustainability and conservation. They promote responsible sourcing and selling of products, particularly when it comes to marine life, in order to protect the fragile ecosystems surrounding the island.

9. Visiting Tips:

When visiting local markets in Zanzibar, it's essential to be respectful of the local culture and bargaining is a common practice. Also, remember to try some street food for an authentic experience, but ensure it's from a reputable vendor to avoid any food safety issues.

In conclusion, local markets in Zanzibar are not only places to shop for goods but also windows into the culture and history of the island. They are integral to the local way of life, serving as economic engines, cultural melting pots, and social gathering spots. Exploring these markets is an enriching experience for anyone visiting Zanzibar.

- *Souvenirs and Crafts*

Zanzibar, an archipelago located off the coast of Tanzania in East Africa, is renowned for its rich cultural heritage and vibrant artistic traditions. Souvenirs and crafts from Zanzibar offer a window into the island's history, culture, and natural beauty. Here, we will explore the diverse range of souvenirs and crafts you can find in Zanzibar.

1. Wooden Carvings: Zanzibar is known for its exquisite wooden carvings, often made from locally sourced materials such as mahogany, ebony, and rosewood. These carvings showcase intricate designs and patterns, and common items include figurines, masks, and furniture. The quality and craftsmanship of these pieces make them popular choices among visitors.

2. Kanga and Kitenge Fabric: Zanzibari women are often seen wearing vibrant and colorful kangas and kitenge fabric. These fabrics are also popular as souvenirs. Kangas are typically rectangular pieces of cloth with elaborate designs and Swahili proverbs, while kitenge is more versatile fabric, used for clothing, bags, and other accessories.

3. Spices: Zanzibar is often referred to as the "Spice Island" due to its history as a major spice producer. You can find a variety of spices such as cloves, cinnamon, nutmeg, and vanilla, often beautifully packaged in local markets. These spices make for both aromatic and practical souvenirs for food enthusiasts.

4. Beaded Jewellery: The island has a thriving tradition of beadwork, with artisans creating beautiful jewellery pieces such as necklaces, bracelets, and earrings. The use of vibrant colours and intricate patterns reflects the lively culture of Zanzibar.

5. Tinga Tinga Art: Tinga Tinga is a unique style of African painting, and you can find these colourful and eye-catching artworks in Zanzibar. Typically depicting scenes from African life and wildlife,

these paintings are great decorative items and unique souvenirs.

6. Swahili Antiques: Zanzibar has a rich history as a trading hub, and it's not uncommon to come across antique items, like brass lamps, old maps, and traditional Swahili furniture, in the markets. These items offer a glimpse into the island's past.

7. Coconut and Palm Products: Zanzibar's tropical climate means an abundance of coconuts and palm trees. Local artisans craft a range of products from these materials, including coconut oil, soaps, woven palm leaf baskets, and mats. These items are both sustainable and practical.

8. Batik Art: Batik is a traditional fabric dyeing technique where intricate patterns are created using wax and colorful dyes. You can find batik artwork and clothing in Zanzibar markets, showcasing beautiful designs inspired by the island's culture and nature.

9. Music and Instruments: Zanzibar is known for its rich musical traditions, and you can often find traditional musical instruments like the oud, drums, and the qanun as souvenirs. These items are

perfect for those interested in the island's music and culture.

10. Seashell Crafts: Given its coastal location, Zanzibar offers a variety of seashell crafts, from jewellery to decorative items. These items reflect the island's natural beauty and the creativity of local artisans.

When shopping for souvenirs and crafts in Zanzibar, it's essential to consider the authenticity and source of the items, as well as bargaining for prices in local markets. Supporting local artisans and businesses not only ensures that you get a genuine piece of Zanzibar's culture but also contributes to the sustainability of the island's traditional crafts.

- Spice Shopping

Spice shopping in Zanzibar is a unique and immersive experience that offers visitors the opportunity to explore the rich history and culture of this island off the coast of Tanzania. Known as the "Spice Island," Zanzibar has been a major hub for spice cultivation and trade for centuries. Here's an overview of spice shopping in Zanzibar:

1. Historical Significance: Zanzibar's spice trade dates back to the 16th century when it was a key player in the global spice trade. Spices like cloves, nutmeg, cinnamon, and black pepper were highly sought after and became central to the island's economy.

2. Spice Farms: The primary way to experience spice shopping in Zanzibar is by visiting one of the many spice farms scattered across the island. These farms offer guided tours where you can see, smell, and taste a wide variety of spices and herbs in their natural habitat. Popular spice farms include Tangawizi Spice Farm and Spice Tour, where you can learn about the cultivation and uses of spices.

3. Diverse Spices: Zanzibar is renowned for producing a wide array of spices, including cloves, vanilla, cardamom, ginger, turmeric, and lemongrass. Each spice has its unique aroma, flavor, and culinary or medicinal uses.

4. Educational Tours: Spice farm tours provide educational insights into how these spices are grown, harvested, and processed. You'll have the opportunity to touch, smell, and taste the raw spices, gaining a deeper understanding of their significance in Zanzibari cuisine.

5. Local Cuisine: Zanzibar's cuisine is heavily influenced by its spice heritage. Many traditional dishes, like pilau rice and biryani, are infused with a blend of spices that give the food a distinct and flavorful taste. You can also purchase freshly ground spices to take back home and use in your own cooking.

6. Souvenirs: Spice farms often have on-site shops where you can purchase a variety of spice-related products. This includes spice mixes, essential oils, handmade soaps, and other unique souvenirs that showcase the island's rich spice culture.

7. Quality and Authenticity: When shopping for spices in Zanzibar, you can be confident of their quality and authenticity. You are buying directly from the source, ensuring that the spices are fresh and unadulterated.

8. Bargaining: Like many marketplaces in the region, bargaining is common when purchasing spices in Zanzibar. Be prepared to haggle to get the best prices, but do so respectfully and in the spirit of the local culture.

9. Sustainability: Many spice farms in Zanzibar promote sustainable and organic farming practices, which is not only good for the environment but also ensures high-quality products.

10. Cultural Immersion: Spice shopping in Zanzibar is not just about buying ingredients; it's an opportunity to immerse yourself in the local culture. You'll meet friendly farmers, learn about their way of life, and gain insight into the significance of spices in Zanzibari traditions.

In conclusion, spice shopping in Zanzibar is a delightful and educational experience that allows you to explore the history, culture, and culinary heritage of the island. It's a sensory journey that you won't want to miss when visiting this enchanting destination.

Chapter 8. Nightlife and Entertainment

- Bars and Clubs

Zanzibar, a semi-autonomous archipelago off the coast of Tanzania in East Africa, is known for its stunning beaches, rich history, and vibrant culture. Bars and clubs in Zanzibar play a significant role in the island's nightlife, offering locals and tourists alike a chance to unwind and enjoy the unique atmosphere of this enchanting destination.

1. Diversity in Nightlife:
   Zanzibar boasts a diverse nightlife scene with options to suit various tastes. Whether you're looking for a quiet beachfront bar to watch the sunset or a lively club for dancing the night away, Zanzibar has it all.

2. Beach Bars:
   Zanzibar is famous for its pristine beaches, and many bars are strategically located along the shoreline. These beach bars offer a relaxed atmosphere with comfortable seating, serving cocktails and fresh seafood. A popular choice for tourists is the Rock Restaurant, perched on a coral outcrop, providing spectacular views and a unique dining experience.

3. Stone Town:

Zanzibar's historic Stone Town is a UNESCO World Heritage site and home to a range of bars. The historic buildings and narrow streets create an intimate setting for visitors. Emerson on Hurumzi's rooftop tea house and bar is a prime example, offering panoramic views and a blend of traditional and contemporary elements.

4. Live Music and Dance Clubs:

If you're in the mood for dancing and live music, Zanzibar has some excellent clubs. Mercury's, inspired by the legendary Freddie Mercury, the lead singer of Queen who was born in Zanzibar, is a popular club in Stone Town. The club often features live music and a lively atmosphere.

5. Cultural Experiences:

Zanzibar's nightlife is also an opportunity to immerse yourself in the local culture. Some bars and clubs host traditional music and dance performances, allowing you to experience the island's unique heritage.

6. Sunset Views:

Many bars in Zanzibar, particularly on the western coast, offer breathtaking sunset views. Whether you're sipping a cocktail at a beachside bar or enjoying a rooftop vantage point in Stone Town, watching the sun dip below the Indian Ocean is a must-do activity.

7. Spice-Infused Drinks:
   Zanzibar is renowned for its spice trade history, and this is reflected in its drinks. You can savor various spiced beverages like cloves and cardamom-infused cocktails that add a distinct local flavor to your night out.

8. Opening Hours:
   Bars and clubs in Zanzibar typically have varying opening hours. Many of them open in the early evening and stay open until late, making it a perfect destination for night owls.

9. Respect Local Customs:
   While Zanzibar is a tourist-friendly destination, it's important to respect local customs and dress modestly when outside of the beach areas.

10. Event Nights:
    Some bars and clubs in Zanzibar host themed nights or special events. It's a good idea to check for upcoming events or promotions before heading out for the night.

In summary, Zanzibar offers a diverse and enchanting nightlife scene that caters to a range of tastes and preferences. Whether you prefer the serene ambiance of beach bars, the historic charm of Stone Town's bars, or the excitement of dance clubs, you'll find an option to enjoy your evenings on this beautiful island. Just remember to immerse yourself in the local culture and respect the customs for a truly memorable experience in Zanzibar's bars and clubs.

- Live Music

Live music in Zanzibar is a vibrant and culturally rich experience that reflects the island's history and diverse influences. Zanzibar, an archipelago off the coast of Tanzania, is renowned for its unique blend of African, Arabian, Indian, and Swahili cultures. This diversity is palpable in its music scene, which offers a captivating fusion of traditional and contemporary genres.

1. Traditional Music: Zanzibar boasts a wealth of traditional music styles, the most prominent being Taarab. Taarab music is a combination of African, Arabic, and Indian elements, characterized by melodious tunes and emotionally charged lyrics. It is often performed with a live ensemble featuring instruments like the oud, qanun, and accordion.

This genre is a testament to the island's historical trade connections and cultural exchange.

2. Sauti za Busara Festival: This annual music festival held in Stone Town, Zanzibar, is a showcase of East African and international music. It features a wide range of genres, from traditional Taarab to reggae, hip-hop, and electronic music. Sauti za Busara has become a celebrated event, drawing both local and international artists and audiences.

3. Live Venues: Zanzibar is dotted with live music venues and bars where visitors can enjoy performances by local musicians. Stone Town, the capital, is particularly known for its vibrant nightlife and live music offerings. Popular venues include Mercury's, the House of Wonders, and the Forodhani Gardens, where you can savor local music and enjoy the backdrop of the Indian Ocean.

4. Local Bands and Artists: Zanzibar has produced numerous talented musicians who perform across the island. Artists like Bi Kidude, Dulla Makabila, and Mim Suleiman have gained recognition both nationally and internationally for their unique musical contributions. These artists often incorporate traditional Zanzibari elements into their contemporary sounds.

5. Influence of Swahili Culture: Swahili culture, deeply rooted in Zanzibar, plays a pivotal role in the island's music. Swahili lyrics and rhythms are a common thread in many local songs, even in genres beyond Taarab. This linguistic and cultural heritage shapes the musical identity of the region.

6. Tourist Attractions: Zanzibar's live music scene is a significant draw for tourists. Visitors have the opportunity to immerse themselves in the local culture through music, and many travel specifically for music festivals and performances.

7. Challenges and Preservation: Despite the popularity of live music in Zanzibar, there are challenges, including the need to preserve traditional music forms in the face of modern influences. Efforts are being made to ensure that the rich musical heritage of the island is passed down to future generations.

In conclusion, live music in Zanzibar is a captivating fusion of cultures, offering a unique and enchanting experience for both locals and tourists. The island's traditional music, contemporary influences, festivals, and local talent all contribute to a thriving and diverse music scene that reflects the rich heritage and vibrant spirit of Zanzibar.

- Festivals and Events

Zanzibar, an archipelago located off the coast of Tanzania in East Africa, is a place of diverse cultural influences, and its festivals and events reflect this rich heritage. Here, we'll explore some of the most significant festivals and events that take place in Zanzibar:

1. Zanzibar International Film Festival (ZIFF):
   ZIFF is one of the most prominent cultural events in Zanzibar. It's an annual film festival that showcases a wide range of international and African films. ZIFF promotes cultural exchange and provides a platform for emerging filmmakers, making it a must-attend event for cinema enthusiasts.

2. Sauti za Busara Music Festival:
   This music festival, often called "Sounds of Wisdom," features a vibrant blend of African music, with artists from across the continent coming to perform. The festival celebrates the diversity of African musical traditions, making it a unique experience for music lovers.

3. Mwaka Kogwa:

Mwaka Kogwa is a traditional celebration held in the village of Makunduchi. It marks the Swahili New Year and is characterized by rituals that include mock fights, singing, and dancing. The festival is a display of Zanzibar's cultural heritage and its deep ties to Swahili culture.

4. Eid al-Fitr and Eid al-Adha:

These Islamic festivals are celebrated with great fervor in Zanzibar. Eid al-Fitr, marking the end of Ramadan, and Eid al-Adha, the Feast of Sacrifice, are significant events for the Muslim population. Families come together for special prayers, feasts, and the exchange of gifts.

5. Zanzibar Revolution Day:

On January 12th, Zanzibar commemorates the Zanzibar Revolution of 1964 when the Sultanate of Zanzibar was overthrown. The day is marked with parades, cultural performances, and political speeches.

6. Stone Town Festival (Sauti za Busara Fringe Festival):

This cultural event showcases Zanzibar's rich heritage with a focus on traditional music, dance, and art. It complements the larger Sauti za Busara

Music Festival and is an excellent opportunity to experience local culture.

7. Zanzibar International Trade Fair (ZITF):
   ZITF is an annual event that promotes trade and commerce in Zanzibar. It provides a platform for businesses to exhibit their products and services, fostering economic development and international cooperation.

8. Zanzibar Food Festival:
   Food enthusiasts can indulge in Zanzibar's culinary delights during this festival. It's a celebration of local flavors and dishes, offering a chance to savor the island's unique cuisine, which is heavily influenced by Arabian, Indian, and African traditions.

9. Zanzibar Beach and Watersports Festival:
   With its stunning beaches and crystal-clear waters, Zanzibar is the perfect setting for water sports and beach events. This festival often includes activities like kite surfing, beach volleyball, and regattas, providing entertainment for both participants and spectators.

These festivals and events in Zanzibar offer a diverse range of experiences, from celebrating its cultural heritage to enjoying its stunning natural beauty. They not only draw tourists from around the world but also serve as an important part of the local culture and economy, making Zanzibar a vibrant and dynamic destination for travelers and enthusiasts of all kinds.

Chapter 9. Practical Information

- *Currency and Banking*

Currency and banking in Zanzibar have undergone significant changes and developments over the years, reflecting the island's unique history and economic evolution. Zanzibar is a semi-autonomous region of Tanzania, and its currency and banking systems are closely intertwined with those of the mainland. Here is an overview of currency and banking in Zanzibar:

1. Historical Background:
   Zanzibar has a rich history as a center for trade and commerce, dating back centuries. The Omani Sultanate heavily influenced the region's culture and economic systems, which included the use of the Maria Theresa Thaler, a popular trade coin in the 18th and 19th centuries.

2. Zanzibari Rufiyaa:
   In the early 1960s, after Zanzibar gained independence from British colonial rule and later merged with mainland Tanganyika to form Tanzania, it briefly introduced its currency, the Zanzibari Rufiyaa. However, this currency was short-lived and replaced by the Tanzanian Shilling

(TZS) as part of the political and economic integration with the mainland.

3. Currency and Banking Today:

Today, Zanzibar uses the Tanzanian Shilling (TZS) as its official currency. This currency is issued and regulated by the Bank of Tanzania, the central bank of the United Republic of Tanzania. Zanzibar has its own branch of the Bank of Tanzania, which operates in Stone Town.

4. Banking Institutions:

Zanzibar is home to various banking institutions, both local and international. These banks provide a wide range of services, including savings and checking accounts, loans, and international currency exchange. Some notable banks in Zanzibar include CRDB Bank, Exim Bank, and Azania Bank.

5. Tourism and Finance:

Zanzibar's economy heavily relies on tourism. The tourism sector has led to the establishment of numerous banks, currency exchange offices, and ATMs, primarily in the urban areas of Zanzibar, such as Stone Town and Nungwi. This infrastructure caters to the needs of both tourists and the local population.

6. Challenges and Opportunities:
   Zanzibar faces challenges in terms of financial inclusion, as many parts of the island, especially in rural areas, still lack access to formal banking services. However, efforts are being made to improve financial literacy and extend banking services to these underserved areas.

7. Regulations and Compliance:
   The banking sector in Zanzibar, like the rest of Tanzania, is subject to regulations and oversight by the Bank of Tanzania. This ensures the stability and integrity of the financial system and compliance with international standards.

8. Foreign Currency Exchange:
   Given its role as a tourist destination, Zanzibar facilitates foreign currency exchange services. Visitors can exchange their currencies at banks, exchange bureaus, or even some hotels. U.S. Dollars, Euros, and British Pounds are commonly accepted and exchanged.

In conclusion, currency and banking in Zanzibar are closely tied to the larger Tanzanian financial system. The island's history, culture, and economy have shaped its monetary landscape, and while Zanzibar uses the Tanzanian Shilling, it maintains a unique identity in terms of its financial institutions and services, especially in the context of its growing tourism industry. The government and the banking sector are working to promote financial inclusion and expand access to financial services across the entire island.

- Communication

Communication in Zanzibar, a semi-autonomous archipelago off the coast of Tanzania, is a complex and dynamic system that plays a crucial role in the daily life and development of the region. This communication can be examined through various lenses, including language, technology, and social aspects.

1. Languages in Zanzibar:
   - Swahili: Swahili is the official language of Zanzibar. It serves as a lingua franca for people of diverse ethnic backgrounds. While Arabic and English are also spoken, Swahili is the most widely used language in everyday communication.
   - Arabic: Due to historical ties with Oman, Arabic holds significance, especially among the Arab community and in religious contexts.
   - English: English is taught in schools and used for administrative purposes, and proficiency varies among the population.

2. Media and Information Flow:
   - Print Media: Zanzibar has a range of newspapers and magazines published in Swahili and English. These media outlets play a crucial role in disseminating information, including news, entertainment, and advertisements.
   - Broadcast Media: Television and radio are popular sources of information and entertainment. Local and international channels are available, making it a vibrant medium for communication.
   - Online Media: The internet and social media have gained prominence, providing platforms for sharing news, ideas, and connecting with the global community.

3. Telecommunications:
   - Mobile Phones: Mobile phone usage is widespread in Zanzibar, with multiple service providers offering a range of services. This has transformed how people communicate, access information, and conduct business.
   - Internet Connectivity: While internet penetration has been on the rise, especially in urban areas, challenges remain, including limited access in rural regions and variations in internet speed and quality.

4. Traditional Communication:
   - Oral Tradition: Storytelling and oral traditions are integral to Zanzibar's cultural identity. Folklore, music, and dance serve as forms of communication, preserving historical narratives and local knowledge.
   - Visual Arts: Zanzibar is known for its artistic heritage, including intricate wood carvings and traditional paintings, which often convey cultural and historical messages.

5. Challenges and Opportunities:
   - Connectivity: Rural areas still face challenges with limited access to modern communication technologies. Expanding infrastructure and improving connectivity is an ongoing concern.
   - Digital Divide: Disparities in internet access and digital literacy exist, impacting access to information and economic opportunities.
   - Cultural Preservation: While modern communication has brought opportunities, there is also a need to balance it with preserving Zanzibar's rich cultural heritage.

6. Cultural Significance:
   - Communication in Zanzibar is deeply intertwined with its rich cultural tapestry. The island's history of trade, migration, and diverse

ethnic groups has shaped its linguistic and communicative diversity.

- Cultural events and festivals are occasions for communities to come together, communicate traditions, and celebrate their shared heritage.

In conclusion, communication in Zanzibar is a multifaceted and evolving landscape, influenced by its historical, cultural, and technological factors. Swahili, the lingua franca, connects the diverse population, while modern technologies and media play a growing role in shaping how information is shared and received. Balancing the opportunities and challenges of modern communication with the preservation of Zanzibar's unique cultural identity remains a key consideration for the region.

- Transportation

Transportation in Zanzibar, an island archipelago off the coast of Tanzania in East Africa, is a vital aspect of the region's economy and daily life. Zanzibar comprises two main islands, Unguja and Pemba, along with several smaller islets. Its transportation infrastructure plays a crucial role in connecting these islands, supporting tourism, and facilitating trade.

1. Road Transportation:

- On Unguja Island, there's a network of paved and unpaved roads that connect various towns and villages. Stone Town, the capital, is a central hub.

- Public transportation consists of minibuses and shared taxis, known as "dala-dalas." These are the primary means of commuting for locals and tourists.

- Car rentals are available for those who prefer more independence.

2. Ferry Services:

- Ferry services are the primary means of traveling between Unguja and Pemba islands. The Zanzibar Ferry Terminal in Stone Town serves as a gateway for these services.

- The Azam Marine and Coastal Fast Ferries are two of the prominent operators providing passenger and cargo ferry services.

3. Air Travel:

- Zanzibar has two airports: Abeid Amani Karume International Airport in Unguja and Pemba Airport. These airports connect the islands to the mainland of Tanzania and other regional destinations.

- Various airlines operate scheduled and charter flights to Zanzibar, making it accessible to international tourists.

4. Boat and Dhow Transportation:
   - Traditional wooden sailing vessels called dhows are still used for inter-island transport and fishing. These dhows are an integral part of Zanzibari culture.
   - Motorized boats and dhows are used for cargo transportation between the islands and the mainland.

5. Tourist Transportation:
   - Zanzibar's tourism industry relies heavily on transportation. Many hotels and resorts offer airport transfers, and there are numerous tour operators offering excursions to different parts of the islands.
   - Tourists can also hire bicycles, scooters, or take guided walking tours to explore the islands.

6. Infrastructure and Development:
   - The Zanzibar government has been investing in improving transportation infrastructure. Efforts have been made to upgrade roads and public transportation, enhancing connectivity.
   - There are ongoing projects to expand and modernize the airports and the Zanzibar Ferry Terminal to accommodate the growing number of tourists and trade activities.

7. Challenges:

  - Congestion in Stone Town and some of the main roads on Unguja is a common issue.

  - Maintenance of roads and bridges, particularly in rural areas, remains a challenge.

  - Ensuring the safety and efficiency of maritime transportation is vital, considering the reliance on ferries and boats.

8. Future Prospects:

  - The Zanzibar government aims to further develop its transportation infrastructure to boost the economy and support tourism.

  - Sustainable and eco-friendly transportation options are being explored to minimize the environmental impact.

In conclusion, transportation in Zanzibar is essential for its economic growth and the well-being of its residents. With ongoing development projects and an increasing focus on sustainability, Zanzibar's transportation system continues to evolve to meet the needs of both its local population and the growing number of tourists visiting this beautiful island archipelago.

- *Local Etiquette*

Local etiquette in Zanzibar, a semi-autonomous archipelago off the coast of Tanzania, is influenced by its unique blend of cultures, including African, Arab, Indian, and European. Understanding and respecting these cultural norms is essential for visitors to have a positive and respectful experience in Zanzibar. Here are some key aspects of local etiquette in Zanzibar:

1. Greeting:
   - When meeting someone, a warm and friendly greeting is customary. A common greeting in Swahili, the local language, is "Jambo" or "Habari" (Hello/How are you?).
   - It's customary to shake hands, but men may also exchange a light hug or pat on the back. However, public displays of affection are discouraged.

2. Clothing:
   - Zanzibar is a predominantly Muslim society, so it's important to dress modestly, especially when visiting mosques and rural areas. Cover your shoulders and knees.
   - At the beach, swimwear is acceptable, but wearing it outside the beach areas is considered disrespectful.

3. Respect for Religion:

- Zanzibar is predominantly Muslim, and you should be mindful of Islamic practices. During prayer times (Salat), it's polite to keep noise levels down and avoid disrupting worshipers.

4. Punctuality:

- Punctuality is valued, but time is often viewed in a more relaxed manner. Don't be surprised if events or meetings start a bit late. It's best to be patient and understanding.

5. Food and Dining:

- When invited to someone's home, it's customary to bring a small gift, such as fruit or sweets, as a token of appreciation.
- Use your right hand for eating and greeting, as the left hand is traditionally considered unclean.
- It's polite to wait for the host to start the meal and to finish everything on your plate.

6. Respect for Elders:

- Elders are highly respected in Zanzibar. When entering a room or a gathering, it's a sign of respect to greet the elders first.

7. Photography:

- Always ask for permission before taking photos of individuals, especially in rural or local areas. Some people may be uncomfortable with their images being captured.

8. Bargaining:
   - Bargaining is common in markets and with street vendors. Be polite and respectful while haggling, and remember that it's a part of the culture.

9. Public Behavior:
   - Public displays of affection should be kept to a minimum, as they are considered inappropriate.
   - Refrain from public drunkenness and excessive use of alcohol. Zanzibar has a conservative attitude toward alcohol.

10. Environmental Awareness:
   - Zanzibar's pristine environment is a treasure. Respect the natural beauty by not littering and disposing of waste properly.

11. Language:
   - Learning a few basic Swahili phrases can go a long way in showing respect and connecting with the locals. Even if your Swahili is minimal, the effort is appreciated.

Remember that Zanzibar is a diverse and culturally rich place, and locals generally appreciate visitors who show an interest in and respect for their culture. Being mindful of these etiquette guidelines will help you have a more enjoyable and meaningful experience while visiting this beautiful island.

Chapter 10. Day Trips and Excursions

- *Prison Island*

Prison Island, also known as Changuu Island or Quarantine Island, is a small, uninhabited island located just off the coast of Zanzibar, a semi-autonomous archipelago of Tanzania in East Africa. It is a place with a rich history and has become a popular tourist attraction, primarily due to its beautiful coral reefs, giant tortoises, and historical significance.

Historical Significance:
Prison Island was originally intended to serve as a quarantine station for the region. In the late 19th century, it was used to isolate and house individuals suffering from deadly diseases such as yellow fever. However, this purpose was never fully realized, and instead, it became a prison for rebellious slaves.

Giant Tortoises:
Perhaps the most iconic aspect of Prison Island is its population of giant Aldabra tortoises. These tortoises were a gift from the British governor of Seychelles, and some of them are over a century old. Visitors can observe, interact with, and feed these gentle giants, which has become a major attraction on the island.

Coral Reefs and Snorkeling:
The crystal-clear waters surrounding Prison Island are home to vibrant coral reefs teeming with marine life. Snorkeling is a popular activity for visitors, who can explore the underwater world, swim among colorful fish, and observe the diverse marine ecosystem. It's an ideal spot for both beginners and experienced snorkelers.

Scenic Beauty:
Apart from its historical significance and wildlife, Prison Island offers stunning natural beauty. The island is covered in lush vegetation, and it provides visitors with picturesque views of the turquoise waters of the Indian Ocean. It's a serene escape from the bustling streets of Zanzibar.

Accessibility:
Prison Island is easily accessible by a short boat ride from Stone Town, the main town on Zanzibar. Many tour operators offer guided trips to the island, which often include snorkeling, tortoise encounters, and the opportunity to explore the island's rich history.

In conclusion, Prison Island in Zanzibar is a unique destination that combines history, natural beauty, and wildlife. Its historical significance, giant tortoises, and pristine coral reefs make it a must-visit attraction for anyone traveling to Zanzibar. It's a place where visitors can learn about the island's complex past, relax on its beautiful beaches, and immerse themselves in the stunning underwater world of the Indian Ocean.

- *Safari Blue*

Safari Blue is a renowned and popular excursion in Zanzibar, an island off the coast of Tanzania in East Africa. This unique experience combines elements of nature, adventure, and cultural exploration, making it a must-do activity for tourists visiting the island. Here is an overview of Safari Blue in Zanzibar:

1. Location: Safari Blue typically departs from Fumba, a fishing village on the southwest coast of Zanzibar. This location is strategically chosen for its proximity to stunning natural attractions.

2. Activities: Safari Blue offers a wide range of activities, making it an all-inclusive adventure. Some of the key activities and experiences include:

   - Snorkeling: Zanzibar boasts crystal-clear waters with vibrant marine life. Safari Blue often includes snorkeling stops at pristine coral reefs, allowing participants to explore the underwater world.

- Dolphin Watching: One of the highlights of Safari Blue is the opportunity to spot and swim with dolphins. Zanzibar's coastal waters are home to bottlenose and humpback dolphins.

- Sandbank Picnic: Safari Blue takes you to a picturesque sandbank in the Indian Ocean. Here, you can relax, sunbathe, and enjoy a sumptuous seafood picnic prepared by the guides.

- Mangrove Forest Exploration: The trip often involves a guided tour through the mangrove forest. You can learn about the unique ecosystem and even take a boat ride through the mangroves.

- Traditional Dhow Sailing: Participants travel on traditional wooden dhows, which adds an authentic and cultural touch to the experience.

- Island Hopping: Depending on the specific Safari Blue package, you might have the chance to visit uninhabited islands like Kwale, Pange, and more.

3. Cuisine: Seafood lovers will be delighted by the delicious seafood served during the Safari Blue picnic. Freshly caught fish, lobster, prawns, octopus, and other local dishes are prepared right on the sandbank, offering a unique culinary experience.

4. Guides and Safety: Safari Blue excursions are typically led by knowledgeable guides who prioritise safety. They provide snorkeling equipment and instructions, ensuring that participants can enjoy the activities safely.

5. What to Bring: Participants are encouraged to bring swimwear, sun protection (hats and sunscreen), a towel, and a waterproof camera to capture the incredible moments.

6. Environmental Conservation: Safari Blue operators are often committed to eco-friendly practices. They educate guests about the importance of preserving the marine environment and avoiding activities harmful to coral reefs and marine life.

7. Booking and Packages: Safari Blue offers various packages, including private charters for couples,

families, or groups. It's advisable to book in advance, especially during peak tourist seasons.

8. Duration: A typical Safari Blue excursion lasts a full day, from morning to late afternoon.

Safari Blue is more than just a tour; it's an immersive experience that combines adventure, nature exploration, cultural insights, and a taste of Zanzibar's vibrant seafood cuisine. It's a remarkable way to discover the natural beauty and cultural richness of this East African paradise.

- Pemba Island

Pemba Island is one of the two main islands of the semi-autonomous archipelago of Zanzibar, located off the coast of Tanzania in East Africa. It is renowned for its unspoiled natural beauty, rich history, and unique cultural heritage. Here, we'll provide an overview of Pemba Island.

Geography and Location:
Pemba Island is situated in the Indian Ocean, about 50 kilometers off the Tanzanian mainland and approximately 80 kilometers northeast of its sister island, Unguja, commonly referred to as Zanzibar. The island covers an area of around 984 square

kilometers, making it the second-largest island in the Zanzibar Archipelago.

Natural Beauty:
Pemba is often called the "Green Island" due to its lush and tropical landscape. It is characterized by dense forests, rolling hills, and pristine beaches. The island's topography is more varied than Unguja, with higher elevations and deep valleys, which contribute to its unique and beautiful scenery.

The island is also known for its rich marine life and coral reefs, making it a popular destination for divers and snorkelers. The Pemba Channel, a deep trench between Pemba and the Tanzanian mainland, is a particularly renowned diving spot with colorful coral formations and a variety of marine species.

Culture and History:
Pemba Island has a diverse and culturally rich heritage. The majority of the population is Muslim, and you can find numerous mosques and Islamic structures throughout the island. The people of Pemba are known for their friendliness and warm hospitality, and they often welcome visitors to experience their local customs and traditions.

Historically, Pemba has a long and complex history, with influences from various civilizations, including the Arab, Persian, and Portuguese. This has left a distinct mark on the architecture, language, and cultural practices of the island.

Economy:
Agriculture is a key component of Pemba's economy. The island is known for its production of cloves, which are a vital export crop. Other crops grown include coconuts, cassava, and tropical fruits. Fishing is also an important economic activity, and the waters around Pemba are teeming with various fish species.

Tourism:
While Pemba Island is less developed for tourism compared to Unguja, it has been gaining popularity as a destination for travelers seeking a quieter and more authentic experience. The island offers a range of activities, from exploring the Ngezi Forest Reserve, a protected area with diverse wildlife, to visiting ancient ruins and historical sites.

Accommodation options on Pemba range from small guesthouses to boutique eco-resorts, with an emphasis on sustainable tourism. The island's tranquility and natural beauty make it an attractive choice for honeymooners, nature enthusiasts, and divers.

Challenges:
Pemba Island, like many other remote regions, faces challenges such as limited infrastructure, access to healthcare, and education. Sustainable development and conservation efforts are important for preserving the island's natural beauty and cultural heritage.

In conclusion, Pemba Island in Zanzibar is a captivating destination with a unique blend of natural beauty, culture, and history. It offers a quieter and more authentic experience compared to its sister island, making it a compelling choice for travelers looking to explore the less-trodden paths of East Africa.

- Mnemba Atoll

Mnemba Atoll, located off the northeastern coast of Zanzibar, is a small coral reef island that has gained worldwide recognition for its stunning natural beauty and thriving marine life. Here, I'll provide an overview of Mnemba Atoll.

1. Location:

Mnemba Atoll is situated approximately 3 kilometers off the northeastern coast of Zanzibar, Tanzania, in the Indian Ocean. It is part of the Zanzibar Archipelago, a semi-autonomous region of Tanzania known for its pristine beaches, rich culture, and diverse marine ecosystems.

2. Geography:
The atoll itself is quite small, measuring only about 1.5 kilometers in length and half a kilometer in width. It is a ring-shaped coral reef surrounding a lagoon, and it's uninhabited, with the exception of a luxurious eco-lodge operated by &Beyond, which occupies a portion of the island.

3. Marine Biodiversity:
Mnemba Atoll is a marine conservation area and a marine reserve. It is known for its incredibly diverse and vibrant marine life. Snorkeling and diving around the atoll reveal a kaleidoscope of coral formations, tropical fish, sea turtles, and other marine creatures. The atoll is home to a wide variety of coral species, which provide essential habitat for countless marine species. It's not uncommon to spot dolphins and humpback whales in the surrounding waters.

4. Conservation Efforts:

Efforts to protect the marine life and coral reefs in the area have been in place for years. Fishing and other potentially damaging activities are restricted to safeguard the fragile ecosystem. The Beyond Mnemba Island Lodge is committed to sustainable tourism and works closely with local authorities to maintain the atoll's ecological balance.

5. Tourism:
Tourism is a major part of the Mnemba Atoll experience. The &Beyond Mnemba Island Lodge offers exclusive accommodations and activities for guests, providing an eco-friendly and luxurious escape for travelers. Activities on the island include snorkeling, diving, birdwatching, and boat excursions. Mnemba Atoll is also a prime location for honeymooners and those looking for a romantic getaway due to its secluded and pristine nature.

6. Accessibility:
Access to Mnemba Atoll is typically through Zanzibar's main island. Visitors arrive at Zanzibar International Airport and then take a boat transfer to the atoll, which is a relatively short journey.

7. Best Time to Visit:
The best time to visit Mnemba Atoll is during the dry season, which runs from June to October. The

calm seas and excellent visibility for diving and snorkeling make this period ideal for experiencing the rich marine life.

In summary, Mnemba Atoll in Zanzibar is a true gem in the Indian Ocean, offering an exclusive and sustainable experience for those looking to explore pristine coral reefs, enjoy the company of diverse marine species, and bask in the natural beauty of this remote paradise. It's a destination that combines luxury with conservation, making it an ideal choice for eco-conscious travelers seeking a unique island escape.

Chapter 11. Language and Culture

- *Swahili Phrases*

Swahili is the official language of Tanzania and Kenya, and it holds particular significance in Zanzibar, a semi-autonomous archipelago off the coast of Tanzania. Swahili, also known as Kiswahili, is not only a widely spoken language in Zanzibar but is deeply embedded in the culture, history, and daily life of the people there. Here's an overview of Swahili phrases in Zanzibar:

1. Greetings and Common Phrases:
   - Jambo or Habari: These are common greetings, with "Jambo" meaning "Hello" and "Habari" meaning "How are you?"
   - Karibu: This means "Welcome" and is often used to greet visitors.
   - Asante: "Thank you."
   - Tafadhali: "Please."

2. Cultural Significance:
   - Swahili in Zanzibar reflects a rich history of trade, blending African, Arabic, and Indian influences. The language carries elements from these cultures.

- It is used in various art forms, including Taarab music, a unique style that combines poetry and song, often in Swahili.
- The Zanzibar International Film Festival showcases Swahili films, which contribute to preserving and promoting the language.

3. Local Dialects:
- There are local dialects of Swahili, with Kiunguja being the most commonly spoken on the Zanzibar archipelago.
- The local dialect may contain some unique phrases and expressions that differ from standard Swahili.

4. Swahili Phrases for Daily Life:
- Nakupenda: "I love you."
- Nashukuru: "I'm grateful."
- Karibu Zanzibar: "Welcome to Zanzibar."
- Napenda chakula cha Zanzibar: "I love Zanzibari food."

5. Business and Trade:
- Swahili plays a vital role in the business and trade sector, especially in Zanzibar's bustling markets.
- Phrases related to bargaining, prices, and quantities are commonly used in the marketplace.

6. Religion and Festivals:
   - Swahili is widely used in religious contexts, particularly during Islamic ceremonies.
   - The festival of Eid is celebrated with Swahili greetings and phrases.

7. Influence on Tourism:
   - As Zanzibar is a popular tourist destination, knowledge of Swahili can be helpful for travelers to communicate with locals and understand the culture.

8. Language Preservation:
   - Efforts are made to preserve and promote Swahili, including in schools and cultural institutions.
   - Zanzibar's government recognizes Swahili as a significant part of its identity.

9. Proverbs and Sayings:
   - Swahili in Zanzibar has a rich collection of proverbs and sayings that reflect the wisdom and values of the local culture.

Swahili in Zanzibar is more than just a language; it's a reflection of the unique history, culture, and way of life in this enchanting island paradise.

Learning a few Swahili phrases can enhance your experience while visiting or interacting with the people of Zanzibar.

- *Local Traditions*

Local traditions in Zanzibar, a semi-autonomous archipelago off the coast of Tanzania, are a rich tapestry of diverse cultural influences, including African, Arab, Indian, and European. These traditions have shaped the identity of the island's inhabitants and contribute to its unique cultural heritage. Here is an overview of some of the key local traditions in Zanzibar:

1. Swahili Culture: Zanzibar's dominant culture is Swahili, a blend of Bantu languages and Arabic. The Swahili people have a distinct way of life, which revolves around the dhow, a traditional wooden sailing vessel used for fishing and trading along the coast. Swahili architecture is also notable, characterized by intricately carved wooden doors and beautiful courtyards in their homes.

2. Spice Trade: Zanzibar is often referred to as the "Spice Island" due to its history as a major center for the cultivation and export of spices, particularly cloves, cinnamon, and nutmeg. Visitors can explore

spice plantations, where they learn about the cultivation and uses of these aromatic ingredients.

3. Music and Dance: Zanzibar boasts a vibrant music and dance scene. The most famous local music style is Taarab, which combines Swahili and Arabic musical influences. It often features a qanun (a traditional Arabic string instrument) and powerful female vocalists. Traditional dances, such as the Beni and Msewe, are also a part of cultural celebrations and weddings.

4. Local Cuisine: Zanzibari cuisine is a delightful fusion of flavors. Influenced by Arab, Indian, and African culinary traditions, it includes dishes like biryani, pilau, and seafood served with coconut rice. The island's street food, including Zanzibar pizza and urojo (a spicy soup), offers a taste of local flavors.

5. Cultural Festivals: Zanzibar hosts various cultural festivals throughout the year, celebrating its diverse heritage. The Zanzibar International Film Festival (ZIFF) is a notable event that showcases African and international films. The Sauti za Busara music festival features African artists and draws crowds from all over the world.

6. Traditional Clothing: Zanzibari clothing is a blend of local and Islamic styles. Women often wear brightly colored kangas, a type of wrap-around cloth, and may cover their heads with a hijab. Men typically wear a kanzu, a flowing robe, especially for formal occasions.

7. Architecture: Zanzibar's architecture reflects its historical connections with the Arab world. The old Stone Town, a UNESCO World Heritage Site, is known for its narrow winding streets, coral stone buildings, and intricately designed wooden doors. These doors are adorned with ornate carvings that tell stories and carry cultural symbolism.

8. Cultural Heritage Sites: Zanzibar is home to various heritage sites that showcase its cultural history. The Sultan's Palace Museum, Old Fort, and the Anglican Cathedral are significant landmarks that provide insights into the island's past.

9. Celebrations and Traditions: Local customs and celebrations in Zanzibar are deeply rooted in Swahili culture. Weddings and rites of passage often involve elaborate ceremonies, traditional music, and feasting. Additionally, Islamic holidays, like Ramadan and Eid, are observed with fasting and special prayers.

10. Language: Swahili is the lingua franca of Zanzibar, but various dialects are spoken across the islands. Arabic is also widely understood and used in religious contexts, as Zanzibar has a significant Muslim population.

In summary, Zanzibar's local traditions are a captivating blend of cultural influences that have evolved over centuries. These traditions encompass language, cuisine, music, dance, architecture, and customs, and they reflect the island's unique history and heritage. Visitors to Zanzibar have the opportunity to immerse themselves in this rich cultural tapestry and gain a deeper understanding of the island's identity.

Chapter 12. Travel Tips and Advice

- *Safety Tips*

Safety is a top priority when traveling to any destination, including Zanzibar, a popular tourist spot known for its stunning beaches and rich cultural heritage. To ensure a safe and enjoyable trip, consider these safety tips:

1. Research Before You Go:
   - Familiarize yourself with the local customs, laws, and culture.
   - Check the latest travel advisories and understand any political or health-related situations in the region.

2. Accommodation Safety:
   - Choose reputable accommodations and read reviews from other travelers.
   - Ensure your lodgings have secure locks and safes for your valuables.

3. Health Precautions:
   - Consult a travel clinic for recommended vaccinations and medications.
   - Carry a basic first-aid kit and any necessary prescription medications.

4. Personal Belongings:
   - Keep your passport, important documents, and money in a secure, waterproof pouch.
   - Use a money belt or hidden pouch to deter pickpocketing.

5. Transportation Safety:
   - Use registered and licensed transportation services.
   - Avoid traveling alone at night, and make sure your vehicle is in good condition.

6. Local Laws and Customs:
   - Respect local customs and dress modestly, especially in more conservative areas.
   - Familiarize yourself with local laws, and obey them to avoid legal issues.

7. Stay Hydrated and Use Sunscreen:
   - Zanzibar can be hot and sunny, so drink plenty of water and apply sunscreen to protect your skin.

8. Swimming and Water Activities:
   - Heed warning signs at the beach, as strong currents can be dangerous.
   - Take snorkelling and diving tours with reputable operators.

9. Food and Water Safety:
   - Drink bottled or purified water.
   - Eat at established restaurants to reduce the risk of foodborne illness.

10. Wildlife Safety:
   - Zanzibar has unique wildlife, and while it's exciting to see, keep a safe distance from animals and follow the advice of guides.

11. Stay in Tourist Areas at Night:
   - Stick to well-lit and populated areas in the evening.

12. Travel Insurance:
   - Purchase travel insurance that covers medical emergencies, trip cancellations, and lost belongings.

13. Emergency Contacts:
   - Keep a list of important phone numbers, including the nearest embassy or consulate and local emergency services.

14. Local Currency:
   - Use official currency exchange services or withdraw money from ATMs located in well-traveled areas.

15. Cultural Sensitivity:
   - Learn a few basic Swahili phrases and show respect for the local culture and traditions.

16. Stay Connected:
   - Carry a charged mobile phone and local SIM card or an international roaming plan for emergencies.

17. Group Tours and Guides:
   - Consider joining group tours or hiring a local guide who knows the area well for added safety and insights.

By following these safety tips, you can enhance your security and peace of mind while enjoying the beauty and culture of Zanzibar. Always be cautious and aware of your surroundings to make the most of your trip while staying safe.

- Itinerary Suggestions

Zanzibar, a semi-autonomous archipelago off the coast of Tanzania in East Africa, is a stunning destination known for its pristine beaches, rich culture, and historical significance. When planning your itinerary for Zanzibar, it's essential to consider the island's diverse attractions. Here are some itinerary suggestions to make the most of your visit to Zanzibar:

Day 1: Arrival in Stone Town
- Arrive at Zanzibar's Abeid Amani Karume International Airport.
- Check into a hotel in Stone Town, the historic heart of Zanzibar.
- Explore the UNESCO World Heritage-listed Stone Town with its narrow winding streets, historic buildings, and bustling markets.
- Visit the House of Wonders, the Old Fort, and the Sultan's Palace Museum.
- Enjoy dinner at a local restaurant with traditional Zanzibari cuisine.

Day 2: Spice Tour and Jozani Forest
- Embark on a spice tour to learn about Zanzibar's famous spice industry.
- Explore the fragrant spice plantations and taste exotic spices like cloves, vanilla, and cinnamon.
- Visit Jozani Chwaka Bay National Park to see the unique Red Colobus Monkeys and diverse wildlife.
- Have lunch at a local restaurant near the park.
- Return to Stone Town for a relaxing evening.

Day 3: Beach Day in Nungwi

- Check out from your Stone Town hotel and head to Nungwi, a pristine beach destination in the north of the island.
- Spend the day swimming, snorkeling, and sunbathing on the white sandy beaches.
- Visit the Nungwi Natural Aquarium or go for a sunset dhow cruise.
- Enjoy fresh seafood for dinner at one of the beachfront restaurants.

Day 4: Diving and Water Activities
- Explore Zanzibar's underwater world with a diving or snorkeling expedition.
- Discover colorful coral reefs and marine life at locations like Mnemba Atoll or Kizimkazi.
- Alternatively, you can go on a fishing excursion.
- Relax on the beach in the afternoon.
- Enjoy another night in Nungwi with beachfront entertainment.

Day 5: Prison Island and Turtle Sanctuary
- Take a boat trip to Prison Island (Changuu Island) to see the historic prison ruins and giant Aldabra tortoises.
- Enjoy swimming and snorkeling around the island.
- Return to Nungwi for more beach relaxation.
- Experience a traditional Zanzibari dinner.

Day 6: Visit Paje and Jambiani
- Check out from Nungwi and head to the eastern
coast of Zanzibar, specifically Paje or Jambiani.
- These areas offer a more laid-back atmosphere
and excellent kitesurfing conditions.
- Try your hand at kitesurfing or simply relax on the
beaches.
- Explore the nearby Rock Restaurant for a unique
dining experience.

Day 7: Cultural and Historical Exploration
- Take a day trip to the nearby village of Kizimkazi
to learn about local culture and traditions.
- Visit the Old Dispensary and the Maruhubi Palace
ruins for historical insight.
- Enjoy a traditional Swahili lunch.
- Spend your last evening in Zanzibar with a
beachside dinner and perhaps a beach bonfire.

Day 8: Departure
- Check out from your accommodation and head
back to the airport for your departure.

Zanzibar offers a diverse range of activities, from
cultural and historical exploration in Stone Town to
beach relaxation and water sports in Nungwi and
Paje. This suggested itinerary covers the island's

most popular attractions, but there are many more hidden gems to discover in Zanzibar, so feel free to adjust your plans to suit your interests and the duration of your stay. Enjoy your trip to this tropical paradise!

Printed in Great Britain
by Amazon

45638842R00089